THE SANCTUARY

This book is dedicated
to the memory of
David Erb

The Sanctuary
Preparing the Church for Worship

Virginia Gosling Mainprize

Illustrated by Willem Hart

Anglican Book Centre
Toronto, Canada

1996
Anglican Book Centre
600 Jarvis Street
Toronto, Ontario
Canada M4Y 2J6

Illustrations, Book design, typesetting: Willem Hart Art & Design Inc.

Canadian Cataloguing in Publication Data

Mainprize, Virginia Gosling
The sanctuary: preparing the church for worship

ISBN 1-55126-096-4

1. Liturgical objects. 2. Church furniture. 3. Altar guilds.
I. Title.

BV195.M35 1996   247   C96-931876-6

Contents

Preface

You may well ask: Another altar guild manual? Why?

Indeed, several manuals for altar workers already exist. However, most are dated, many are incomplete, and few are Canadian. *The Sanctuary* is a comprehensive book about the history and use of church furnishings and their care and preparation for church services. It incorporates the liturgical changes introduced by *The Book of Alternative Services* while remaining appropriate for *The Book of Common Prayer*.

The Sanctuary is not a how-to manual which gives altar guild workers definitive directions for preparing for the services of their parish. There is no bible for altar guilds. Liturgies change, worship committees try new practices, priests in charge have their own methods; so, there is neither one way nor an unchanging way for altar work. Local style, custom, taste, and budget determine how worship will be conducted. This book provides a basis for a parish to devise its own preparation for worship, be it traditional or contemporary, simple or elaborate.

The Sanctuary is divided into four sections. The first, Background and Customs, examines the history and organization of altar guilds, the liturgical year and its symbolism, and the history and use of the church building. This section should enable new altar guild members to feel more at home in their workplace.

The second section, Furnishings: Their Use and Care, identifies those articles whose maintenance and preparation are the altar guild's responsibility. Guidelines and checklists for the care and preparation of furniture, vessels, linens, vestments, candles, and flowers are provided at the end of each subsection and should be adapted to the needs of each guild.

Services: The Setting Up is the third section. Here, altar guild members will find a guide for preparing the furnishings for church liturgies. Again, suggestions and checklists are provided and should be adapted.

The fourth section of appendices contains a service of initiation, bread recipes, prayers, and suggestions for further readings.

It is hoped that the information *The Sanctuary* contains will be as useful to those who work in small mission churches as to those who minister in large diocesan cathedrals.

Acknowledgements

This book could not have been written without the help and support of many kind people who took time from busy schedules to read the manuscript and offer advice and suggestions. I am enormously grateful to Charlotte Ambridge, Ruth Baillie, Danny Bishop, Ann Dalzell, the Reverend Brian Freeland, the Reverend Paul Gibson, Sister Helena SSJD, the Reverend Roy Hoult, the Reverend Paul Maclean, the Reverend David Smart, and to Karen Evans and Caese Levo at the library at Anglican Church House.

Introduction

In worship, we give ultimate value to something we believe to be of absolute worth. Free or formal, private or corporate, worship is a human response to a Divine Mystery so enormous that when we stand in its presence we are both delighted and awed.

Liturgy is the community's expression of worship, an evolving demonstration of its awareness of its relationship with God. We Christians use ritual and symbol to express our faith in the God revealed to us in the life, death, and resurrection of Jesus Christ.

Although the essence of Christian liturgy remains the same, liturgical practices have been changing throughout the church's history. They began with the simple gatherings of the first Christians and moved to the elaborate focus on physical things in the late middle ages. The Reformation simplified worship, and today we are recovering the breaking of bread as the centre of our worshipping lives. And as our liturgies have changed and evolved, so have the appointments for those liturgies and the way we use them.

Even though we may regularly attend the various liturgies of the church, many of us are unaware of the work that is involved in preparation. We may not even think about the behind-the-scenes organization, assuming that somehow, by some miracle, the table is set, the vestments are laid out, and the housekeeping is done. However, in each parish and church, no matter how large or small, simple or elaborate, rich or poor, someone is doing the housekeeping. In today's church, it is a dedicated group known as the altar guild or the chancel guild or altar workers.

Background and customs

Altar guilds past and present

The origins of altar guild work go back to the earliest days of the church. When the first Christians gathered together to break bread at each other's houses, it was the responsibility of the host family to make the arrangements for the meal.

History of altar guild work

As the number of Christians grew and the church became institutionalized, these house eucharists were celebrated in larger buildings. These places for meeting and worship, and the items in them, needed care. The *Apostolic Tradition* of Hippolytus, written around A.D. 215 in Rome, assigns this work to specific individuals: the building to the doorkeeper, the vessels to the subdeacon, and the books to the lector.

Subsequently, these responsibilities were given to sacristans — men in minor orders in the church. Minor orders were abolished by the Church of England at the Reformation, and the parish clerk took over these duties. Later, supervising the sacristy, preparing for worship, and caring for the church and church paraphernalia became the responsibility of a lay sacristan, generally assisted by a group of women completely responsible to him. Gradually, these women assumed many of the sacristan's housekeeping tasks, and eventually they organized themselves into groups known as parish altar guilds.

Until recently, these guilds were usually made up of pious women of excellent reputation who were not employed outside the home. If they had families, the children were either grown and could look after themselves or were looked after by servants. These women were expected to make great sacrifices of their time looking after the church's housekeeping. Rigorous training and an apprenticeship of six months to a year were obligatory. Appropriate behaviour was strictly defined — the women were required to keep quiet while working, to cover their head, and to wear a smock. A manual for altar guild workers written by Edith Weir Perry and published in 1934 stressed that "the more self-effacing a member is, the more valuable she is." It was expected that members place the "love of Christ above all personal feeling [and that they work] together in perfect agreement and peace."

Although circumstances have changed over the centuries, the essence of altar guild work has remained constant. Preparation for the eucharist and the other sacraments and offices of the church, and care of the altar, sanctuary, vessels, and vestments are "behind-the-scenes" jobs necessary for the efficient functioning of worship.

However, altar guild work should not be regarded as mere housekeeping. It may seem to be menial work, but, because *laborare est orare* (to work is to pray), it is done for the greater glory of God. Care for the furnishings of a church supports the liturgical life of a parish. It is a vital ministry and a great privilege.

Altar guilds today
Until recently, guild work was the only way that women could serve God at the altar. Today, changes in society and in the church have introduced a change in the membership of altar guilds.

In many Canadian Anglican parishes, altar guild work is still done primarily by the women of the community. However, altar guilds are no longer the terrain of matronly or maiden ladies as they often were at the beginning of this century. Today, duties are shared by women of all ages and backgrounds — those who work at home, those who work outside the home, students, and those who are retired. In some churches, guilds include men and even entire families. As our awareness of the nature and importance of lay ministry continues to grow, it is encouraging that this work, so essential for the conduct of public worship, is becoming a ministry of all of the people of God.

The priest and the altar guild
The purpose of the altar guild is to assist the priest and other worship leaders run worship smoothly. The priest is the *ex officio* head of the altar guild; however, he or she usually appoints someone else to be in charge. This director will oversee the work of the guild and will consult regularly with the priest. The director should be a person who is responsible, organized, and works well with others and, particularly, with the priest. Other guild officers — such as secretary, treasurer, and flower secretary — are sometimes appointed. Specific skills may be valuable in altar work, but the most important requirement is a sense of responsibility, loyalty, and humour.

The organization of altar guilds
People's busy lives make efficient scheduling of altar guild duties essential: no longer can all members be on call, nor can they always come regularly. Some

people can spare only a few hours once a month or even a few times a year. Guild members may not be free on a weekday or even on a Saturday morning, the time traditionally set aside for most altar guild work. So schedules should be flexible to allow people to do altar work when they have the time. The director should take into consideration the talents of the members, not assigning tasks to those who have no interest or skill in performing them. There are people who iron badly; however, they may be happy to launder the towels and cloths used for cleaning. Some people get great satisfaction from polishing brass and can do this work which others would avoid at all cost; while still others, who are talented at needlework, might be asked to repair old linens and sew new ones.

Flexible, efficient scheduling should be accompanied by good training. Altar guild members should know what the various pieces of church paraphernalia are and how they are used. They should be aware of the structure and meaning of the services. Good organization and good training ensure that altar guild members are not waiting for someone to tell them what to do, but can arrange their work efficiently. They can come at odd hours, at times convenient for them, and do their work without supervision.

The organization of each altar guild is a local matter. It depends on the size of the parish and the guild, the number of services that are held, the nature of those services, parish tradition, and the preferences of the priest in charge.

A convenient way of organizing the altar guild is to assign members to teams, each with a captain who oversees the group's work. Each team is given a week of duty, usually once a month. The members may then be given specific duties, such as laying out the vestments, or arranging the flowers, or polishing all the brass. The captain checks to see that all the tasks have been completed.

In some churches it is customary for the guild members to meet on Saturday mornings to prepare for the following Sunday's eucharist. In others, where members have schedules and commitments that prevent them from gathering as a group, individual members attend to their responsibilities whenever they can spare the time.

Duty rosters remind members of their duties and help keep track of whether or not these tasks have been completed. Some guilds post these rosters in the sacristy and ask members to sign them when they are finished their work. Other guilds may ask members to fill out the list themselves.

Becoming and being an altar guild member
There is a service to initiate altar guild members into their ministry — the Commissioning for Lay Ministries in the Church — in *Occasional Celebrations* which may be used as it appears or adapted. This rite may take place during the regular Sunday service or at another time. At a eucharist, the commissioning

follows the homily and creed; at Morning or Evening Prayer, it takes place before the intercessions and Thanksgivings. It is appropriate that it be done on the chancel steps. (See Appendix 1 for the initiation service from *Occasional Celebrations*.)

Altar guild meetings should be held regularly so that members get to know each other, have an opportunity to discuss and deal with their concerns, and can talk to their priest about worries. The priest and the director of the altar guild should be present, as should the guild secretary taking minutes of the meeting. Meetings begin with either a eucharist or prayer for the work of the guild, and the purposes of the guild may be read out loud.

All altar work should begin with brief private prayer, dedicating the work to the greater glory of God and to the enhancement of the worship. A suitable prayer may be the last verse of Psalm 19: "Let the words of my mouth and the meditation of my heart be acceptable in your sight, O Lord, my strength and my redeemer." (See Appendix 2 for more prayers.)

Sample duty list

DATE	SERVICE	DUTY	MEMBER	SIGNATURE

The church year

History

The church year is arranged so that in our readings, prayer, and worship we can remember the Christian mystery — the Jewish experience of God's holiness and liberating power; the incarnation of Jesus, his life, death, and resurrection; and the coming of the Holy Spirit to the church.

By the late first century, Sunday, the first day of the week, had become the weekly memorial of Christ's resurrection. No feasts were observed. In the second century, Easter, associated with the feast of Pascha or Passover, was the only feast. It was not only an observance of Christ's death but also a celebration of the mystery of Christ, including the incarnation, resurrection, and glorification. The celebration consisted of a vigil and a eucharist on the day itself. Later, Easter was preceded by a period of prayer and fasting originating from the custom of preparing candidates for baptism at Easter. In the fourth century, the liturgical re-enactment of the last days of Jesus' life on earth, Holy Week, began in the Jerusalem church. The events were commemorated on the traditional sites at the approximate original times. This commemoration spread to other churches, and Holy Week became a part of the church's fixed calendar. The celebration of the Christmas season also began in the fourth century.

Today, the church year includes the Sundays, the principal feasts, the holy days, days of special devotion, and days of optional observance. The calendars of the church year are found in *The Book of Common Prayer* (pages ix–xii) and *The Book of Alternative Services* (pages 14–33). Each Sunday, the day that Christians gather to celebrate in word and sacrament the mystery of Christ, is the Lord's Day and, as such, takes precedence over saints' days. Only principal feast days and a few other feasts supersede the normal Sunday celebration (see *The Book of Alternative Services*, page 15).

Advent

The church year begins with the first Sunday of Advent, always four Sundays before Christmas. It is the Sunday nearest the feast of St Andrew (November 30) who was, as explained in John 1: 40–42, the first of Jesus' disciples. Advent commemorates the beginning of Jesus' public mission to the world. The season ends on Christmas Eve.

The penitential and joyful tones of the Advent liturgies were formed by several Christian traditions: anticipation of the birth of Jesus Christ; preparation for new life in Christ; and mindfulness of the second coming of Christ and of the reign of God. Advent today is the church's new year season. Coming near the time of the Celtic Samhain (November 1) which was the Celtic new year,

Advent wreath

the season has incorporated aspects of renewal and spiritual preparation which, in the northern hemisphere, characterize this period of lengthening nights and dwindling days.

In some Anglican churches, an Advent wreath is displayed and its candles are lit each Sunday. This custom came to us from the Lutheran church of Scandinavia and originated in pre-Christian ceremonies of light at the time of the winter solstice. The use of the wreath among Anglicans in modern times was part of a movement to encourage family prayers. Sometimes wreaths were placed in churches and were lit each Sunday to model appropriate use in the home. Today in many parishes, the presence of the wreath has become the norm. Altar workers usually set it up and trim the candles.

Christmas

The Christmas season begins with the first evensong of Christmas and continues for twelve days. The last day of the Christmas season is the feast of the Epiphany on January 6. If January 1, the feast of the Naming of Jesus, known as the Octave Day of Christmas or the Circumcision of our Lord in *The Book of Common Prayer*, falls on a Sunday, it takes precedence over the Sunday.

Christmas is a season of joyous celebration. Unfortunately, it can also be a time of frenetic activity for altar guilds. In the same way that we should try to avoid being overcome by the externals of the celebration and the busyness of the time of year, those doing the preparatory work for Christmas liturgies should try not to forget the true meaning of this celebration. Careful organization, meticulous scheduling, and the sharing of responsibilities are particularly necessary at this and other busy times in the church's liturgical calendar. The decoration of the church and the cleaning of the brass can be an opportunity to co-opt extra helpers from the parish, especially young people, and may incorporate an element of social conviviality.

The Feast of the Epiphany

The origin of this feast was the Eastern celebration of the birth and the baptism of Jesus. At the end of the fourth century, when the Eastern church adopted the feast of Christmas to celebrate the incarnation, Epiphany continued to celebrate the Lord's baptism. However, in the west, Epiphany became the commemoration of the coming of the magi and the manifestation of Christ to the Gentiles. Epiphany (also known as Twelfth Night) is celebrated on January 6, twelve days after Christmas.

The Greek letters Chi and Rho are the initials of Jesus Christ

In *The Book of Alternative Services*, the first Sunday after Epiphany celebrates the major feast of the Baptism of the Lord and is particularly appropriate for baptisms. The Presentation of the Lord (Candlemas) is celebrated on February 2 and takes precedence over the Sunday.

The last day of this season is the Tuesday before Ash Wednesday known as Shrove Tuesday. Ash Wednesday is the first day of Lent. In *The Book of Common Prayer* the three Sundays before Ash Wednesday look forward to Lent rather than back at Epiphany. Their formidable names, Septuagesima, Sexagesima, and Quinquagesima, mean the seventieth, sixtieth, and fiftieth day before Easter; but only Quinquagesima is accurate. The other two are approximations.

Lent

The forty days of Lent are a time of penitence, reconciliation, and prayer. The season grew out of a period of intensive preparation in the fourth-century church for the baptism of new Christians at the Great Vigil of Easter. Other members of the community joined the baptismal candidates during this time of instruction, prayer, and fasting in preparation for the celebration of Christ's resurrection. Later,

Crucifix

Palm Sunday

Lent became a time when people who had been disciplined for grave sin prepared for their restoration at Easter. By the tenth century, Lent had become a time of personal penitence, symbolized by the imposition of ashes on Ash Wednesday. The ashes used to mark a sign of the cross on the foreheads of the faithful are prepared by burning the palm fronds and palm crosses of the previous year's Palm Sunday (Sunday of the Passion). Today, the imposition of ashes is optional.

Because Lent is a time of austerity, it is customary in some parishes to do without flowers during the season; to cover statuary, pictures, and brass crosses with unbleached or rough cloth; and to replace brass crosses with wood. However, since the forty days of Lent do not include the six Sundays, some churches feel that the use of flowers on those Sundays is appropriate, especially on the fourth Sunday when some parishes celebrate Mothering Sunday.

The collects, prayers, and prefaces for Lent exhort the faithful to ask God for forgiveness, to follow Jesus' example of prayer and fasting, and to renew their lives in the paschal mystery. The feasts of St Joseph (March 19) and the Annunciation (March 25, Lady Day) are the only ones celebrated in Lent, and they do not take precedence over Sunday. If they fall on a Sunday, they are transferred to the preceding Saturday or to a day in the preceding week. If the Annunciation falls in Holy Week, it is transferred to the week after Easter. Some parishes may celebrate Passion Sunday on the fifth Sunday in Lent and may veil the processional and the altar crosses until Maundy Thursday.

Holy Week

Holy Week, the final week of Lent, includes the liturgical re-enactment of the events of the last days of Jesus' life. The commemoration of Holy Week originated in Jerusalem in the fourth century. Holy Week begins on the Sunday of the Passion (called

Palm Sunday in *The Book of Common Prayer*) and ends with the Easter Vigil. *The Book of Alternative Services* provides liturgies as well as propers for each day of the week, including the major days of the Sunday of the Passion, Maundy Thursday, and Good Friday.

This is a busy time for those preparing the sanctuary. On the Sunday of the Passion (Palm Sunday), palms or branches of other trees or shrubs may be placed in vases, and palms and palm crosses may be distributed at the service and carried in procession.

Maundy Thursday commemorates the institution of the Lord's Supper. Its name comes from the Latin *mandatum novum*, "a new commandment" (John 13:34). At the Maundy Thursday eucharist, all lenten symbols are usually removed, and the sanctuary and altar are decorated as for a festival. Vestments, altar frontals, and church hangings are traditionally white or red. At the conclusion of the liturgy, which can include the washing of feet, the altar may be stripped and washed. All vessels, frontals, crosses, candles, and banners may be removed and put in the sacristy, and sanctuary lamps may be extinguished. This work is done by the celebrant and vested servers, and members of the congregation and altar guild members may help. The origins of this practice are not liturgical but enable the altar guild to clean vessels and appointments for Easter. In some parishes, the sacrament may be taken to an altar of repose where it will remain until the Good Friday liturgy. On Good Friday, the day commemorating the crucifixion and death of Jesus, the altar remains stripped. It is a tradition in some churches that the eucharist is not celebrated on this day and any communion is administered from the reserved sacrament. However, *The Book of Alternative Services* provides a liturgy both for eucharistic celebration and for communion using reserved elements.

Foot washing, a Maundy Thursday ritual

Easter

The celebration of the season of Easter begins with

Lilies are the traditional flowers for Easter

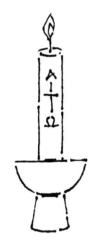

The paschal candle

the Great Vigil of Easter and ends with Pentecost. In the early church, Easter was the only Christian festival besides Sunday. It lasted fifty days from the Vigil until Pentecost and celebrated the death and victory of our Lord and his sending of the Holy Spirit. In the course of time, the "death" element of the Vigil was moved back to Good Friday. It was then a logical step to move the celebration of the Last Supper to the night before. The original unity of these elements can be seen in *The Book of Alternative Services* which has no dismissal at the end of the Maundy Thursday and Good Friday rites because the liturgy will not be concluded until the first eucharist of Easter has brought the Vigil to its climax.

The Great Vigil of Easter, the first service of Easter in *The Book of Alternative Services*, is celebrated between sunset on Holy Saturday and sunrise on Easter morning. It is a glorious service used by more and more churches today; its liturgy is filled with ancient symbolism, with joy, and with the spirit of renewal. It normally consists of four parts.

The first part is the Service of Light during which the paschal candle is lit from the new fire. The candle, which symbolizes both Christ the light of the world and the pillar of cloud by day and the pillar of fire by night which led the Hebrews, is carried in procession through the darkened church to the middle of the sanctuary. If members of the congregation have been given candles, these are lit from the paschal candle. Other candles and lamps are also lit, except for those on the altar. Altar guild members, as well as servers, may have a part in this.

The service continues with the Liturgy of the Word, during which at least three sections from the Old Testament (one of which, the passage from Exodus 14, is never to be omitted) and two from the New Testament are read. The readings are followed by a rite of thanksgiving over the water and the baptism of candidates (if there are any). Whether or not there are baptisms, members of the congregation renew their baptismal covenant and may be sprinkled with blessed water. The altar is then lit with the maximum number of candles, floral arrangements are brought out, antependia and banners may be displayed. The service ends with the celebration of the eucharist and the Easter communion.

The feast of the Ascension of our Lord is celebrated forty days after Easter. The day is a Thursday and may be the occasion of a mid-week eucharist in the early evening. The season of Easter ends with the great feast of Pentecost or Whitsunday.

Traditional symbol for St Matthew

The Feast of Pentecost

In Jewish custom, Pentecost, the feast of the harvest and the commemoration of the giving of the law to Moses at Mount Sinai, was celebrated fifty days after Passover. Today in the Christian year, Pentecost celebrates the coming of the Holy Spirit, the fulfilment of the promises of Easter, and the birthday of the church.

There are no particular liturgical celebrations associated with Pentecost other than the lighting of the paschal candle for the last time and moving it to the baptistry. In *The Book of Common Prayer* calendar, Pentecost ends on its octave, known as Trinity Sunday. Between Trinity and Advent, *The Book of Common Prayer* calendar celebrates the feasts of St Barnabas, the Nativity of St John the Baptist, St Peter and St Paul, St Mary Magdalene, St James the Apostle, the Transfiguration of our Lord, St Bartholemew, Holy Cross, St Matthew, St Michael and All Angels, St Luke, St Simon, St Jude the apostle, and St Jude, the brother of the Lord, All Saints' Day, and St Andrew. In *The Book of Alternative Services* calendar, Pentecost is followed by "ordinary time" which extends to Advent and commemorates the continuing work of Christ in his church through the Holy Spirit. During this period, the following feasts are celebrated: the Sunday of the Trinity, St Barnabas, the Birth of St John the Baptist, St Peter and St. Paul,

Traditional symbol for St Mark

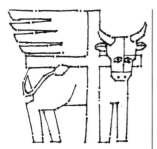

Traditional symbol for
St Luke

Traditional symbol for
St John

St Thomas, St Mary Magdalene, St James, St Stephen, the Transfiguration of the Lord, St Mary the Virgin, St Bartholemew, the Beheading of St John the Baptist, Holy Cross Day, St Matthew, St Michael and All Angels, St Luke, St Simon and St Jude, All Saints, and St Andrew, all of which take precedence over the Sunday if they fall on that day.

As this "ordinary time" includes the whole of the summer vacation season, it can necessitate considerable adjustments in altar guild scheduling. But it can also provide an opportunity for reviewing procedures, taking stock of supplies, and planning for the autumn. Training sessions can be initiated as personal schedules may be less hectic. Long-term projects of needlework or embroidery can be undertaken. For many altar guilds, the celebration of Harvest Thanksgiving may be the first occasion for major decorative activities after the calm of summer.

Liturgical colours

History
In most Anglican churches today, vestments and altar hangings of specific colours are used on different occasions and for different seasons. However, no rubric or canon in the Anglican Church of Canada specifies the use of particular colours for vestments and church decorations. Those mentioned in the *Order of Divine Service* and on church calendars are suggestions congruent with general use.

The association of colours with seasons and occasions has historical and psychological roots. In the early church, liturgical vesture was white, the same as civilian dress. The first-known specified colours come from the Augustinian canons in Jerusalem, which strangely enough called for the use of black at Christmas and the feasts of Mary, and blue for Epiphany and Ascension. It was not until the sixteenth century, after the Catholic Reformation and the introduction of the missal of 1570, that the "traditional" colours were defined in the Roman Catholic rubrics — white for joyous festivals, red for feasts of the Holy Spirit or for martyrs, violet for penitence, black for the departed, and green for other occasions. But local custom persisted for a long time, and it was only in the nineteenth century that "traditional colours" were universally adopted in the Roman church.

Although the Reformation abolished the use of coloured vestments in the Church of England, some clergy continued to wear coloured copes and even chasubles. However, it was only with the Catholic revival of the late nineteenth and early twentieth centuries that some Anglicans adopted the post-Reformation Roman colour system. Some English cathedrals continued to use their own unique seasonal and commemorative colours. Today, the liturgical movement has created an atmosphere where the colour scheme is increasingly adaptable, and some parishes are using colours that may be more suitable for their building or more symbolic of their culture than the suggested ones.

Symbolism
White, in some cultures, symbolizes purity and joy and may be used on the great festivals commemorating Christ's life, for the feasts of Mary the Virgin and certain saints, for All Saints, and for Trinity Sunday. Gold may often be substituted for white.

Red is the traditional colour of the fire of the Holy Spirit and the blood of martyrdom and may be used for all festivals of the Holy Spirit, for the feasts of martyrs, and sometimes during Holy Week. Shades of red may differ, from fire red to blood red. Red also may be used for the ordination of priests and the consecration of bishops, although white is often preferred in contemporary rites.

Green, the colour of most growing things, may symbolize life. It can be used during the season of Epiphany and the season after Pentecost to reflect an emphasis on Christian life.

Because purple dye was the most expensive, the colour purple was used by emperors and kings. It is a royal colour that reminds Christians of the promised victory over death. The colour has come also to symbolize prayer, penitence, and sorrow. It is the colour used during Lent and Advent in some churches. Rose vestments, seen as a less sombre form of purple, are used, by churches that have them, on Advent III (*Gaudate* Sunday) and Lent IV (*Laetare* Sunday).

Blue, an ancient liturgical colour, symbolizes truth and eternity and may be used for penitential preparation. In many churches, blue is replacing purple as the colour of Advent.

Black, which symbolizes death and mourning and was for a long time the traditional colour used at funerals, is being used less frequently today.

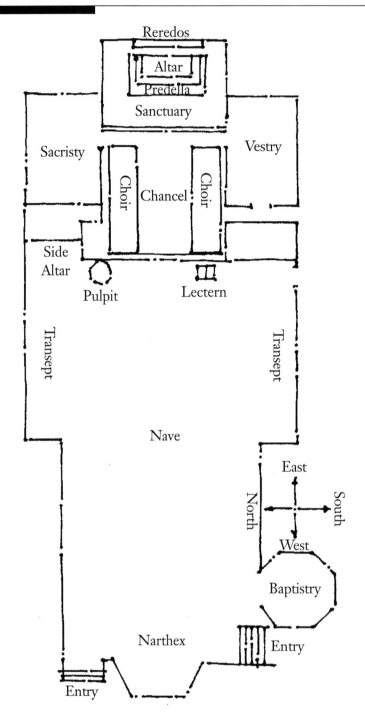

Floor plan of a traditional cruciform church

The church building

History

Since preparation for church services takes place throughout the building, altar guild members should be able to recognize and identify its parts.

Over the centuries, church architecture has evolved as a result of changes in styles of worship and in taste; however, the basic features have remained constant. Large or small, ancient or modern, traditional or contemporary, simple or elaborate, church buildings possess three common elements: an altar or holy table for the celebration, a baptismal font symbolizing new life in Christ, and a place for the proclamation of the word.

During the Gothic Revival of the nineteenth century, medieval forms, which had suited the worship of the later middle ages, were revived. Deep chancels, into which the choir was moved, separated the altar from the people; the longer altars of the baroque period were reintroduced; and candles and crosses were put either on or above the altar. Today, there is a movement in some parishes to place the altar closer to or among the community, to move the font into the midst of the people, to provide more space for processions, and to move the site of the liturgy of the word closer to the congregation.

The parts

The **narthex** is the vestibule or entrance. In early churches, it was the transition space between the secular and the sacred and was the place where catechumens and penitents remained during the liturgies. Today, this area, depending on its size, provides a place where sidesmen can greet and hand out leaflets and books to those coming into the church. It can have a bulletin board for notices, a rack for pamphlets, and a place for the visitors' book. The new fire may be lit there at the Easter Vigil, and it is a place where church processions may begin. In traditional churches, the baptismal font is either in or near the narthex.

Beyond the narthex is the **nave** or the main body of the church. Worshippers gather there to hear the word and, depending on the practice of the parish, remain for the celebration of the eucharist. In traditional church architecture, the nave has a passage through the centre and similar passages at the sides. The nave may have fixed pews facing the altar or partially or completely surrounding it, or it may have seats that can be moved about.

The **chancel** in traditionally designed churches contains the sanctuary and altar, and seats for the ministers and the choir. In the medieval church, the chancel was often separated from the people by a chancel screen. A raised **pulpit** may stand on the left side as one faces the altar. From it the gospel may be read and the sermon may be delivered. On the other side of the chancel, there may be a

lectern for the reading of the lessons. In some churches, the sermon, the gospel, and the lections may be delivered from the middle of the chancel or in the nave, and a portable lectern may be used for all the readings.

It is common for the choir in Victorian-style churches to sit on either side of the chancel between the nave and the altar; however, the choir may also sit at the back of the church, in a gallery or at the side. Beyond the choir and separated from it by an altar rail is the **sanctuary**. Here, raised on a **predella** or "foot-pace" with steps leading up to it, stands the **altar**, the focal point of eucharistic worship. In recently built or renovated churches, one may see a free-standing altar with or without a communion rail, or an altar in the centre of the building surrounded by pews or chairs, the style of the churches of the first millennium of Christianity.

Somewhere close to the sanctuary is the **sacristy**, the room where the vessels and vestments for the services are kept and the preparation for and the clean-up after the services are done. It may also be the room where priests and servers come to dress for the service, although in many churches they may do this in a separate room — the **vestry**.

Furnishings: their use and care

The sacristy

The centre of most altar guild work is the sacristy. It is usually close to the sanctuary. Some churches have only a very small workroom; others have wonderfully designed sacristies filled with drawers of various depths, many cupboards, lots of counter space. There may be two rooms, a working sacristy and a vestry with cupboards for storing vestments. Because some churches have no sacristy at all, some very ingenious places and methods for preparing for church services have been improvised.

No matter how simple or elaborate the sacristy, it is important that altar guild members become familiar with its layout and learn where things are kept. A detailed explanation of the sacristy and its contents is the best introduction to altar work for each new member. An individual session with an experienced worker is more effective than a group tour. This introduction should be followed by several working sessions during which the new member becomes more acquainted with the sacristy's setup and is initiated gradually into altar guild duties and routines.

Organizing the sacristy

An inventory of all the items in the sacristy is necessary; photographing vessels, linens, vestments, and hangings is an easy way to keep a record and is invaluable for insurance purposes. Everything stored in the sacristy should have its own clearly labelled place. Master charts, displaying the contents of drawers and cupboards, assure that everything is returned to its assigned place and can leter be found.

Checklists for members taking home linen for laundering (see page 50), and duty rosters for those doing daily, weekly, and occasional work (see page 16) keep track of who is doing what, when. Church calendars inform workers quickly about the colour of the day. Charts showing the vesting of a chalice (see page 68), the laying out of vestments (see page 71), and the placement of the vessels (see page 68) are reminders of correct procedures. A guide sheet for stain removal (see page 49) tells how to remove stains from linens and vestments. A shopping list reminds members what supplies are needed. A bulletin board for notices is also useful, and a directory of all altar guild members with their telephone numbers should be posted. If members of the congregation or the guild supply the bread for the eucharist, their names may also be recorded. A flower chart is an invaluable way of keeping track of what flowers are needed, when they should be ordered, and in whose memory they are presented (see page 64). Good stock taking, running inventories, careful documentation, efficient organization, and lists and more lists are important for the smooth operation of the altar guild.

The keeping of coherent records of who gave what, when, and in memory of whom is invaluable for the parish history. If the parish has a computer, lists can be kept on a database or spreadsheet, together with other pertinent material (place and date of purchase, value, scheduled replacement date for items such as candles, wine, etc.), and updated regularly. All this cataloguing and listing may seem daunting, but it can be done gradually by guild members who can spare the time. It will pay off.

The well-planned and well-equipped sacristy has a few basic requirements. It should have drawers of various depths and sizes, plenty of closets and cupboards, and a safe or locked cupboard for valuables. Ample counter space and a good-sized work table are invaluable. Hot and cold water and a sink are helpful. In some parishes the rinsing water for vessels and linens that have touched consecrated elements is not poured down the drain into a sewage system but onto the ground. In this case, there may be two sinks — one, a general purpose sink; the other, a **piscina** which drains directly into the ground. If there is no piscina, a separate bowl or basin may be used, and the rinsing water poured outside onto the ground.

Checklist for the sacristy
The following is a list of the items that a well-stocked

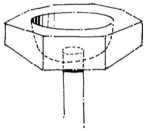

A piscina which drains directly into the ground

sacristy might have. Some are essential, some optional, others a luxury.

1. An electric kettle to boil water for rinsing the chalice and ciborium, melting wax, and removing certain stains from linens (not to mention preparing all-important cups of tea while relaxing after work).

2. A vacuum cleaner, mops, brooms, dustpans, and dust cloths.

3. Towels of various sizes, some reserved exclusively for wiping and drying the vessels. Towel drying racks.

4. A generous supply of cloths, paper towels, sponges, and dishcloths.

5. Plastic basins for rinsing, soaking, and washing.

6. A waste basket and a large garbage bin; garbage bags. Some churches have a recycling bin for empty bottles and paper.

7. An ironing board and a good steam iron for light touch ups to linens and vestments, even if laundering is done in members' homes.

8. Cleaning supplies, including dish soap, laundry soap, prewash, bleach, baking soda, turpentine, paint thinner, peroxide, ammonia, sink cleaner, steel wool, and all-purpose cleaner. A bottle of club soda and salt for removing certain stains.

9. Silver and brass polish with soft rags for polishing, and treated mitts for touch-up jobs. Furniture polish. Vinegar and denture cleaner for removing sediment from, and adding lustre to, crystal and glass.

10. Flannel bags for storing silver and brass.

11. A bread box or sealed container for storing hosts and bread.

12. Flower arranging equipment: containers of various sizes and colour and of various materials, tins and cake tins painted a dark colour to be placed inside them; flower scissors, a sharp knife, and a vegetable peeler; rolls of two-inch and one-inch wire netting; blocks of foam known by the trade name Oasis; plastic bags of a number of sizes and sheets of plastic or drop sheets; string and wool; buckets, a watering can with a long spout, and a

misting can, pinholders at least 3 inches (7.5 cm) in diameter; florist's tape and wire, scotch tape, strong elastic bands, wax, twist ties, newspaper, tissue paper; coarse sand and a few heavy stones; and a small funnel.

13. A sewing kit with needles, thread to match vestment colours, pins (straight and safety), buttons, thimble, and tape measure. Two or three pairs of scissors of different sizes.

14. Matches and a lighter in a metal container with a tight-fitting lid.

15. A tool kit containing a screwdriver with changeable heads, wrench, hammer, small nails, and thumb tacks.

16. A first-aid kit.

17. Paring knives, a small funnel, a corkscrew, bottle stoppers, a measuring cup, and spoons.

18. Brown paper and blotting paper for removing wax from carpets and linens.

19. A clock, pencil and paper, scotch tape, masking tape, a church calendar, and a bulletin board for notices, charts, and duty rosters. Labelling material and a "post-it" note pad.

20. Hangers, both padded and regular. A dressmaker's dummy.

21. Acid-free tissue paper, plastic and cloth garment bags, a garment brush.

22. Multiple sets of rubber gloves, hand soap, hand towels, a nail brush, and hand cream.

23. A fire extinguisher. A fireproof metal sheet or stone slab where the thurible may be prepared. Tongs for charcoal. A hook or stand on which to hang the thurible. Aluminium foil to line the thurible.

24. A full-length mirror if the sacristy is used as the vestry.

25. A card for suitable prayers. (See Appendix 2).

26. A small reference library (see Appendix 4).

Sanctuary furniture

History

In the early church, worship was organized around the Sunday eucharist. The community gathered together and, after the greeting, "The Lord be with you," listened to selections from the Old and the New Testaments and from the psalms, read from a reading desk or *ambo* by the lector. Then, the celebrant preached the sermon sitting down, and the prayers of intercession followed. The people's offerings of bread and wine were brought forward; enough for all to share was placed on a table covered with a white cloth and often put in place only at this point in the service.

Today's sanctuary furnishings are very similar to the furniture of those early gatherings — a table for the celebration of the eucharist, another table to hold extra vessels, a pulpit or lectern, and chairs for the celebrant and for those assisting. Only a few other items have been added, and their purpose too is functional.

The furniture

Altars may be elaborately carved and decorated or unadorned, small or large, of costly or simple material, depending on the history and tradition, local taste, and budget of the congregation. But each altar, whatever its size or decoration, is a holy table, the centre of the church's worship.

Many altars today are free standing so that the celebrant may face the people. Some, "altars in the round," are in the centre of the nave, surrounded by the congregation. The position of the altar can dictate the style of altar covering (see page 44 — hangings). The top of the altar, known as the **mensa**, may be marked with five crosses symbolizing the five wounds of Christ. **Altar rails**, unknown in England before the Reformation, may separate the sanctuary from the rest of the chancel. Originally they protected the altar in churches where dogs roamed freely. Today, they may be used by people kneeling to receive communion. In churches where people stand during the distribution of bread and wine, altar rails may be eliminated altogether.

A custom introduced in the late medieval church and again revived in current Anglicanism is the placing of a cross on or above the altar. This may be an undecorated **cross**, a **Christus Rex** with the figure of Christ wearing royal robes and a golden crown, or a **crucifix**. A crucifix is a cross with the figure of the dead or dying Christ. Until the fourteenth century, the figure of Christ was portrayed as triumphant, the face turned towards heaven (*Christus triumphans*). Later, the suffering Christ of the crucifixion (*Christus patiens*) was portrayed.

In larger churches and cathedrals, especially of the nineteenth-century Gothic

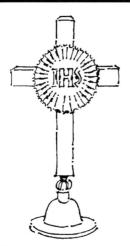

Altar cross with the IHS symbol, the first Greek letters of Jesus

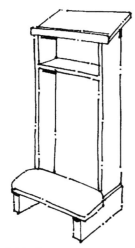

A prie-dieu

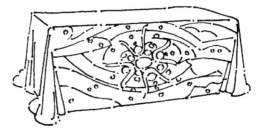

*Altar with a Laudian frontal**

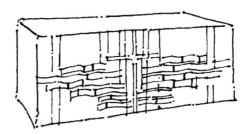

*Altar with a Jacobean frontal**

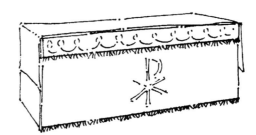

Altar with a traditional frontal and frontlet

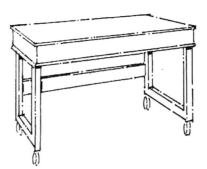

A moveable altar

*Both designs are by Helen Fitzgerald for Grace Church-on-the-Hill, Toronto.

Revival period, there may be a **reredos** behind the altar. This tall screen of wood or stone is elaborately carved with figures from the Old and New Testaments, with Christian symbols, or with the tablets of the law, the creeds, or the Lord's Prayer. Sometimes, especially in churches where the altar is still affixed to the wall and the celebrant faces away from the people, a long, heavy curtain or **dossal**, in the colour of the church season, replaces the reredos.

Behind the free-standing altar in many churches is a small shelf or table called the **gradine** or **retable** which was originally part of the reredos. A tabernacle, office lights, and sometimes flowers may be on the gradine which may be used as a credence table.

The **credence table**, usually on the right side of the altar as one faces it, holds extra chalices, cruets, the bread box, and the lavabo bowl and towel. Before the eucharist, a second credence table may be set out at the back of the nave to hold the elements to be carried in the offertory procession. The **tabernacle** is a box for the reserved sacrament, the consecrated bread and wine put aside to take to the sick. It may be lined with white linen or satin and may be vested to match the colour of the altar hangings. The **aumbry** (which is more common than the tabernacle these days) is a small cupboard set in the wall and used for the same purpose.

In the sanctuary, against the side walls, are chairs or benches, known as **sedilia**, that are used by the officiating clergy and servers. A **prie-dieu**, an individual kneeler with a reading desk, may be placed in front of the chairs and benches. There may also be stands and shelves for the altar book, which in some churches is not brought to the altar until the offertory, for other books, and the alms basin.

Care of the furniture
In some parishes, the altar guild may be responsible for dusting and polishing the furniture. A good quality paste wax, applied sparingly and not too often, gives a more durable finish than spray waxes. Altar rails, lecterns, and pulpits, which tend to show hand and finger prints and need to be cleaned frequently, may be wiped down with a slightly damp cloth or sprayed lightly with furniture polish, and dried and buffed with a clean cloth.

Sacred vessels

History
In the earliest days of the church, people brought their offerings of bread and wine and other gifts to the altar in their own vessels. Later, churches began to

collect beautiful and elaborate vessels for the eucharist, often the gift of generous patrons.

In the later middle ages, when the laity no longer received the cup, the chalice became smaller. The Reformation churches restored communion in both kinds and a larger chalice. However, with the reintroduction of the wafer and the administering of less wine during Victorian times, the chalice again became smaller and the flagon was replaced by cruets.

Today, more and more churches are moving away from the practices of nineteenth-century Anglicanism and returning to older traditions. The vested chalice and priest's host are less frequently found on the altar at the beginning of the eucharist or later, when placed there by the celebrant. Instead, the bread and wine may be carried to the altar by members of the congregation after the liturgy of the word. Appropriate containers are baskets, trays, or plates for the bread, and decanters, carafes, jugs, or pitchers for the wine.

The vessels

The **chalice** is the cup used to hold and distribute the wine. It may be made of gold, silver, pewter, glass, ceramic, or even wood. It is customary that only one chalice be on the altar during the consecration of the elements. If extra chalices are used, each is covered with a purificator and left on the credence table until after the breaking of the bread. Then, these chalices are brought to the altar to be filled.

The **ciborium**, a chalice-like vessel with a lid, may be used to hold the wafers at the eucharist. It dates from the ninth century when eucharistic piety fostered concern for the tiniest fragment of consecrated bread. The people rarely received communion, wafers replaced bread, wine was no longer administered to the laity, and the ciborium replaced the large plate-like paten. If the ciborium is used today, it is placed, before the eucharist, either on the sanctuary credence table or the credence table at the back of the church

Chalice

Ciborium

to be carried to the altar at the offertory. Communion may be distributed from the ciborium or from a paten or basket.

Paten

The **paten**, usually made of the same material as the chalice, is a plate which holds the priest's wafer. With the substitution of wafers for bread in the middle ages, patens became smaller. They became larger again after the Reformation when leavened bread was reintroduced, but with the revival of the wafer in the late nineteenth century, the smaller medieval paten reappeared. If a loaf of bread is used instead of wafers, it can be placed on a larger plate or in a basket, covered with a white cloth or corporal.

Cruets of glass, crystal, metal, or pottery hold the wine and the water. An extra cruet or **lavabo jug** may hold the water for the washing of the celebrant's hands. **Flagons** are much larger than cruets and are used at services where more wine is needed. A round or square **bread box** contains extra wafers and usually sits on the credence table. The **lavabo** is a small bowl, also placed on the credence table, over which the celebrant washes his or her fingers. This custom dates from a period when the priest received all sorts of gifts from the people at the offertory and washing the hands was essential. Today, some priests have dispensed with this custom, although many have retained it as a symbol of reverence for the presence of Christ in the bread.

Flagon

Cruet

Other hardware and furnishings
Over the centuries, a number of other appointments came into common usage. Many churches still use these items regularly; others, responding to the move to simplification, may have them stored away; others, because of their own tradition or because of a limited budget, may not have them at all.

Lavabo bowl, cruet, and towel

Most parishes have **plates** of brass, silver, wicker, or wood to collect the offering. Those carried to the pews are smaller and less elaborate than the **alms basin** which receives the collection when it is brought

Bread box

Thurible and incense boat

Sanctus bells

Snuffer

Missal stand with altar book and markers

to the altar at the offertory. A large **pitcher** or **ewer** of brass, glass, silver, or pottery holds water for baptism and for the foot washing ceremony on Maundy Thursday.

The use of incense dates back to the fourth century in Christian tradition, but far earlier in Hebrew ceremonies. Incense offerings were burned every morning and evening by the priest in the Jewish temple. The early church rejected the use of incense because of its association with incense offerings to the pagan gods and the Roman emperor, but the custom was re-introduced after the legalization of Christianity. It is optional in today's churches. Sweet grass may be used instead of incense, and both may be burned over charcoal in a **stationary censer** or in a **thurible** (a metal vase with a pierced cover) which is swung in the hand or suspended by chains. A **boat** is the small vessel holding the incense which is ladled onto the burning coals with a matching **spoon**.

Traditionally used to alert the congregation to the focal points of the eucharist, the ringing of **sanctus bells** is still a custom in some churches. The bell or bells are placed on the floor at the epistle side of the altar (the right side when one faces it) and may be rung at the Sanctus, the elevation, and the priest's communion. **Candle snuffers**, usually of brass, hold a waxed taper to light candles. The snuffers quickly get coated with black wax and soot, and require frequent cleaning to avoid drips.

During the entrance, and in some churches at the gospel and the offertory procession, an acolyte known as the crucifer may carry the **processional cross**. It may be preceded or flanked by two torchbearers carrying candles.

A large altar book, containing the services and the propers, is placed on the altar, either on a **pillow** or on a **missal stand** made of brass, silver, or wood. Altar guild members are sometimes responsible for placing markers in the book, indicating the propers and parts of the liturgy. Some books have permanent tabs placed at the edge of the page to mark some of these places.

The **monstrance**, which only a few churches still use, derives from the medieval ritual of the adoration of the blessed sacrament. The consecrated host is placed in a sunburst in the centre of a standing cross. The monstrance is placed on the altar for veneration or is carried in procession during solemn benediction. Also not in general use is the **asperges bucket** which holds holy water that is ceremonially sprinkled with the **aspergillium**. In some parishes, a **warden's wand**, a tall stick with a silver or gilt top — mitre-shaped for the rector's warden and crown-shaped for the people's warden — is placed beside each warden's pew (where the wardens may or may not sit) or is carried by them in procession.

Asperges bucket with aspergillium

The care and setting up of a **Christmas crèche** may be entrusted to the altar workers in many parishes, as is the setting up of an **Advent wreath.**

There are other items which may be stored in the sacristy but are not used in liturgies held in the church building. When visiting the sick, the priest carries the blessed sacrament in a **pyx**, either a double pyx when the sacrament is reserved in both kinds, or a small round box which is sometimes attached to a chain so it can be worn around the neck. The **oil stock** is a small cylindrical container with a top that screws on; it carries the anointing oil.

Advent wreath

Care of vessels

Because silver polish wears away metal, only the best quality silver polish should be used, sparingly and very occasionally. Otherwise, vessels may be washed with warm, soapy water, rinsed clean, and polished with a soft cloth while they are still warm. With regular washing and rubbing most vessels remain untarnished. They may be stored in individual flannel bags.

Pyx and oil stock

Brass, on the other hand, needs to be polished each time it is used. A thin film of brass polish is applied and rubbed off immediately. Brass polish can be thinned with water for easier application and removal, especially when cleaning ornate pieces. To get rid of the build-up of polish which can seriously dull brass, wipe the object with turpentine or varsol (using a soft brush or cotton swab to get into the cracks), or wash it in warm, soapy water and rinse well. Lacquering brass and silver is not recommended because it causes yellowing, and the lacquer tends to chip or peel. If lacquered items need cleaning, they can be rubbed with a very soft cloth. Brass polish dissolves lacquer and should never be used on lacquered brass. Lacquer can be taken off with a paint remover for enamel-based paints, but this should be done using rubber gloves in a ventilated area other than the sacristy.

Crystal and glass vessels should be emptied as soon as possible after each service. Normally, they are simply washed in warm, soapy water, rinsed clean, and wiped dry with a linen cloth. Film deposits can be removed by filling the vessel with warm vinegar and letting it stand for a few hours, or by filling it with water and dropping in a tablet of denture cleaner. This method is faster than using vinegar and leaves the glass fresh and sparkling. To prevent mildew, cruets are stored without their stoppers or corks inserted.

Cleaning the thurible
The bowl of the thurible may be lined with double or triple layers of aluminium foil to facilitate the removal of coal ashes and to decrease tar build-up. A cup can be used as a mold to shape the foil. Cleaning the thurible is difficult because the incense is actually baked onto the inside surface. Some parishes have devised ingenious ways of dealing with this problem. The thurible may be sprayed with standard oven cleaner in a ventilated area and left to stand in a large enamel roasting pan. The cleaner may be removed with a paper towel or an old cloth, and the thurible is washed and then polished with silver or brass polish if necessary. Another simple and effective method is

Assemble the following:
A large bowl or old pot of suitable size to accommodate the thurible.
A paring knife.
Old scrubbing brushes.
A large container of paint thinner.
An empty container marked "Dirty Paint Thinner."
Plastic to cover the work surface (could be a garbage bag).
Rubber gloves.
Newspaper, soap, cloths.
Appropriate metal cleaner. Screw driver.

1. Remove the foil cup that has lined the thurible bowl.

2. Submerge the thurible in paint thinner in the pot or bowl and leave for a while. In some parishes, the thurible is soaked until preparation for the next service takes place. The used paint thinner can be poured into a container and used again and again. (The thurible may be soaked instead in a solution of baking soda and water in which a piece of aluminium foil has been placed. A chemical reaction takes place, and after a few days the tar deposits soften for easy removal.)

3. Brush the thurible and its chains, removing the tar.

4. Wash the thurible in hot, soapy water.

5. Clean and polish the thurible using the appropriate metal cleaner.

6. Untangle the chains, place a foil cup inside the thurible, and hang it up, ready to be used.

Checklist for cleaning vessels
Silver — Avoid using silver polish too often. Wash the silver with warm, soapy water, rinse clean, and polish with a soft cloth.

Brass — Use brass cleaner thinned with water. Rub it off immediately and polish with a soft cloth. Turpentine or varsol may be used to get rid of polish build-up.

Glass and crystal — Wash in warm, soapy water as soon as possible after use. Rinse clean and wipe dry. Vinegar or denture cleaner may be used to dissolve sediment.

Church linens

History
The term "church linens" describes not only white linen cloths but also all covers and cloths used in the church and at the altar. The only cloth specified by the rubrics of both *The Book of Common Prayer* and *The Book of Alternative Services* is a clean white cloth, the fair linen, to cover the altar during the eucharist. The use of a tablecloth can be documented as early as the second century. The holy table was bare until the offertory when the deacon spread a cloth on the altar. After it became customary to leave the cloth (the fair linen) on the altar at all times, a second cloth (the corporal, a placemat in effect) was placed under the

chalice to protect the under cloth. It was large enough to be draped over the chalice to protect it from insects and dust. Later a second corporal, the origin of today's pall, covered the chalice. Small cloths called purificators are used to wipe the cup during the eucharist. The corporals and purificators may be kept in a burse, a case placed on top of the chalice.

Today's linens

The **cere cloth** may cover the top of the altar and was originally used to protect the fair linen from condensation that formed on top of stone altars. It is not always used in today's heated churches; however, it protects the mensa from getting stained. It was traditionally made of a heavily waxed, waterproof cloth but today may be either flannelette or plastic. It is cut to fit the mensa exactly and is not hemmed.

The **fair linen** covers the cere cloth, either fitting the top of the altar or hanging down at the sides. It may be embroidered on the top with five crosses, one in each corner and one in the centre, symbolizing the five wounds of Christ. The overhanging edges may be embroidered or are sometimes edged with lace. For services other than the eucharist, a white cloth, known as a **prayer cloth**, may cover and protect the fair linen. When the altar is not in use, it is covered by a **protector** or **dust cover**, made either of white linen or coloured material. This may fit the top of the altar exactly or hang over to protect the sides of the fair linen.

A piece of medium-weight, white linen about 20 inches (50 cm) square, known as a **corporal**, is placed under the chalice before or during the offertory. It is an attenuated version of the larger *palla corporalis* which was used on the altars of the earlier centuries and was drawn up over the chalice. Today, the corporal protects the fair linen and catches particles of bread or drops of wine. Before and after the liturgy, it is folded to form nine squares, first in thirds and again in thirds, embroidered side up, and may be held in a case known as the burse. The corporal is decorated with a cross embroidered in the centre third at the bottom edge or sometimes in the centre.

The Book of Common Prayer rubric specifies that a second corporal cover the chalice and paten if they contain remains of the consecrated elements to be consumed after the end of the eucharist. The custom may apply in *The Book of Alternative Services* rite even if there is no rubric to direct it. Alternatively, the **chalice pall**, a piece of linen tightly sewn over a piece of plexiglass or cardboard, may replace this corporal.

A square linen napkin, smaller than the corporal and known as a **purificator**, is used to wipe the chalice after each communicant drinks from it, and later to wipe the chalice and paten after the communion. At the beginning of the eucharist, it is draped over the top of the chalice. Additional purificators may be kept in the burse or on the extra chalices at the credence table. Purificators are usually embroidered with a Greek cross, either in the centre or in the lower right-hand corner.

A small **lavabo towel**, often made of more absorbent material, is used during the eucharist to wipe the priest's fingers after he or she washes them. It is folded and placed across the lavabo bowl. **Baptismal towels**, used to wipe the foreheads of the newly baptized, are very similar to lavabo towels and are sometimes distinguished by an embroidered shell.

Not really linens and usually matching the colours of the day, a **burse** and **veil** may be used to cover the chalice at the beginning of the eucharist. The veil is draped over the chalice, and the burse, which holds the corporal and the purificators, is placed on top. (see page 68 for a chart showing the traditional vesting of a chalice.) The burse and veil are used less often today.

Linen cloths, known as **credence cloths**, cover the credence and other tables, and are usually stored on cardboard rollers to minimize creasing. An **aumbry veil** of fine material may hang inside the door of the aumbry, covering the opening; and the aumbry may be lined, like the tabernacle.

Hangings
The earliest permanent altar covering was an unadorned silk cloth which dropped to the floor on all sides. During the eucharist, only a white cloth and the bread and wine were placed on it. In time, as altars decayed and it was cheaper to cover than replace them, they were draped with coverings of brocade and damask, heavily embroidered and even incorporating precious stones. When the altar was pushed against the wall in medieval times, it was no longer necessary to cover all sides. The cloth, still as

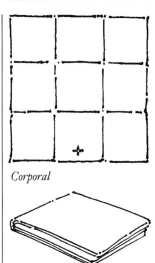
Corporal

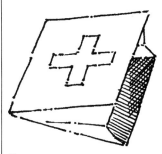
Lavabo towel

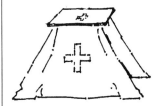
Burse

Burse and vail

elaborately decorated, covered the front of the altar only. This custom continues today in many churches.

The front of the altar may be covered by a **frontal** which just touches the floor. It is usually made of heavy material and may be elaborately decorated; its colour may match that of the day. Frontals are attached to the altar by hooks or a rod, or they are mounted on a frame which is moveable. The upper part of the frontal may be covered by a **frontlet** (superfrontal) of the same fabric and design, or a frontlet alone may be used. It is sewn to a piece of coarse linen which fits over the mensa and under the fair linen. Free-standing altars are sometimes draped with a Jacobean frontal which covers the whole altar like a tablecloth. A Laudian frontal is in the same style as the Jacobean but is fitted at the corners. If either a Jacobean or Laudian frontal is used, the fair linen usually covers only the top of the altar and does not hang down the sides.

Altar stoles are strips of material of no specified width which hang from the front of the altar or from the front to the back, about three-quarters of the way to the floor. They may be used in churches which have a single frontal of a neutral-coloured material. These stoles, made of coloured fabric, plain or embroidered, may be changed to indicate the season or feast.

A square or oblong piece of silk, which often matches the colour of the day and is known as the **fall** or **antependium**, may hang from the prayer desk, the pulpit, the lectern, and a prie-dieu. Long strips of material, which may match the other hangings, mark the books — **Bible markers** for the Bible and **missal markers** for the altar book.

At funerals, requiem eucharists, or commemorative services, the **funeral pall** covers the coffin. For a member of the armed forces, a flag may be used instead. At memorial services, either may be used to cover the catafalque, a bier representing the absent coffin. For services after cremation, a white veil, which may

*Altar with a Laudian frontal**

Altar with a traditional frontal and frontlet

Funeral pall designed by Doris McCarthy for Grace Church-on-the-Hill, Toronto

be embroidered or decorated with lace, is draped over the urn which is otherwise treated liturgically as a bier. The container is placed on a small table covered with a white cloth.

Banners may be on permanent display in a church, or they may be used only during processions and kept in the sacristy. **Wedding cushions**, usually of white satin or needlepoint, are kept in the sacristy and are used as kneelers for the bride and groom during the wedding service. During Lent, some churches follow the custom of covering the statues, crosses, and pictures with **lenten veils** of unbleached voile or rough cloth; some cover them from Passion Sunday (Lent V) or only in Holy Week with purple, white, black, or red cloths.

The care and storage of linens
Fabric
Since altar linens play such an important part in most of the liturgies of the Anglican church, and since fine-quality embroidered linens are very expensive, it is important that they be looked after carefully. Proper laundering, ironing, mending, and storage are certainly worth the effort.

Not all altar linens need to be made of the finest linen; there are some practical, economical synthetics and synthetic blends on the market that are quite satisfactory. However, they are not recommended for corporals and purificators. These cloths, especially purificators, may come in contact with wine and lipstick which may be cleaned from pure linen but are extremely difficult to remove from synthetic material. As well, purificators should absorb water easily when the priest is using them to cleanse the vessels at the ablutions. "Permanent press" material is acceptable for fair linens and credence cloths where neat appearance is desirable and there is less likelihood of stain. Purificators and lavabo and baptismal towels also may be made of diaper, birdseye, or huckaback.

Washing
Another departure from tradition is the use of washing machines to launder church linen. Today's machines have temperature and agitation speed controls which allow them to wash even the most delicate materials. A third departure from tradition is that today, unlike in the past when all members of a guild were expected to do their share of laundering, this task is usually given to those with the skill and the interest. Many people, both men and women, find laundering and ironing satisfying work; others loathe it and are hopelessly inefficient at it. Their talents can be used in other ways.

Altar linenes will need attention immediately after they are used. When purificators are returned to the sacristy after the eucharist, they are usually in the chalice. They have been used to wipe out the chalice after the communion and have absorbed some of the consecrated wine, and they may also be lipstick stained.

In some churches, any remnants of the consecrated elements are disposed of down the piscina or directly onto the ground. First, boiling water from an electric kettle is poured into the chalice over the purificators. Then, the purificators are dropped into the piscina or a basin. More boiling water is swirled around the edges of the chalice and poured over the purificators. They are then shaken out, any stains are treated with a prewash detergent, and the purificators are placed in a bowl of cool water. Any crumbs on the corporal may be shaken into the piscina or basin as well (the water from the basin is poured outside onto the ground). This procedure ensures that any wine and crumbs still in the chalice or on the linen do not go down into the sewer system. Some parishes do not follow this practice and wash linens used during the eucharist in the same way as other linens.

After this preliminary care, linens can be washed by hand or on the gentle, cool cycle of the washing machine, using a mild soap. It is important that they be rinsed until the water is clear, and some suggest the addition of a cup of white vinegar to remove any residual soap. Chalice palls, if they are made of plexiglass, do not need to be unstitched to be washed; they can be washed by hand in warm, soapy water, rinsed, and then stood upright to dry.

Stain Removal

Certain difficult stains need special treatment. Lipstick stains can be removed by soaking the linen in club soda for a while or using a prewash spray, but perhaps the most effective treatment is to apply undiluted liquid detergent to the spot and rub it gently. If none of these methods works, the linen may be soaked carefully in peroxide mixed half and half with ammonia. Chlorine bleach should not be used or used sparingly, for it tends to shorten the life of the linen and may leave spots and eventually yellow the fabric. An excellent method of restoring linen to snowy brightness is to lay it in the sun, still damp. This method can, however, damage fabrics in time as well.

Wine is the next greatest bane of those who look after altar linens. Salt may be placed on the stain if it is still wet; club soda may be poured on the linen if the stain is dry. Alternatively, the linen can be treated with a prewash detergent, or boiling water can be poured through the stain while the cloth is stretched over a bowl. The linen should be washed in the usual way after the stain has been treated.

Rust is a less common stain. It can, however, be difficult to remove. Wet the linen with lemon juice and rub salt into the rust stain. Dry the linen in the sun if possible, and then rinse it in an ammonia-water solution and wash it using a mild detergent. Light mildew can be removed by normal washing and sun drying, or by soaking the linen in peroxide for a few minutes. Soot, ash, and smoke stains may be rubbed with detergent (after the ash has been shaken loose or touched lightly with masking tape if shaking or blowing doesn't work), and then the linen is washed in the regular way. Candle wax may be be scraped off with a dull implement, or a brown paper bag may be placed over the spot and ironed using the cotton setting. Then the greasy stain is treated with a commercial degreaser, mild cleaning fluid, or turpentine. Another method of removing wax is to dip the waxy spot in Varsol and rub it gently until the wax is dissolved. The linen is then washed in hot soapy water and rinsed well.

Drying and Ironing

Altar linens should not be dried in the clothes dryer on the hot cycle for this will damage the fibres. Linens may be wrapped in a towel, allowed to stand for about an hour at room temperature or a couple of hours in the refrigerator, and then ironed. To prevent scorching, the iron should not be too hot. Heavy cotton and linen damask may be ironed on high heat, but lighter weight linens and synthetics are pressed with only a warm iron. Lace linens may be ironed between two cloths to keep the threads from being crushed or torn. To iron embroidery, place one or two layers of a terry towel under the embroidered cloth and iron on the wrong side. Not only does the embroidery look better, but it lasts longer. Iron the rest of the piece on the right side to bring up the gloss. Because ironing-in folds increases the wear on linens, they should not be folded until they are quite dry, and then the folds should not be pressed in.

Corporals are ironed flat and folded wrong side out. When they are quite dry, with the embroidered side up, the lower third is folded up first, then the upper third is folded down over it. The right third is then folded to the centre, and finally the left third is

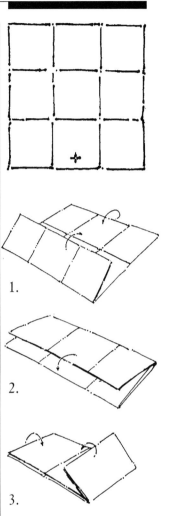

1.

2.

3.

Corporals are ironed flat and folded embroidered side up. The lower third is folded up (1) and the upper third is folded over it (2). The process is repeated first from the right (3) and then from the left until the corporal is folded into nine squares.

folded inwards, so that the corporal is folded into nine squares. The folding of the purificator follows the same steps except that it is folded embroidered side down, so that the third with the embroidered cross ends up on top. Lavabo and baptismal towels are folded first into thirds and then in half, with the cross on top.

Laundering and ironing the fair linen for the holy table is a huge task, and in many parishes it is done by a professional dry cleaner. If it is done by guild members, the linen is washed by hand or in the washing machine on the cool, gentle cycle in a mesh bag to prevent the linen from twisting. Ironing is ideally a two-person job. One person irons while the second supports the freshly ironed length. If a second person is not available, a long plastic sheet can be placed on the floor and the ironed portion of the fair linen is advanced along it. A painless way of ironing fair linen is to iron it face down, roll up the ironed part onto a wide roller, unroll it little by little, iron it face up, and roll it back onto the roller. If the linen is still even slightly damp, it should be unrolled, placed on a flat surface to air, and then rolled again. Then it is ready to unroll face up on the altar. To ensure that the fair linen lies straight on the altar, the side hems should not be stretched. After it has been ironed, the credence cloth is also stored onto a roller with the embroidered side on the inside.

If linens cannot be ironed immediately after washing, they can be taken, still damp, from the washer, folded or rolled up, wrapped in plastic, and put in the freezer. Frozen linens can be taken out to thaw the day before ironing or can be put in a microwave oven at high setting for a few minutes and turned to ensure that they are completely thawed. They should remain damp for easier ironing. Touch-ups can be made to wrinkles on larger linens by placing a towel under the linen, dampening the creased area, and pressing with a hot iron. This work can be done with an unplugged, well-heated iron.

Linens should not be stored in plastic because the fabrics may mildew. Nor should they be wrapped in ordinary tissue paper which contains acids that may spot the fabric; however, acid-free tissue can be used. Linens should be stored in a cool, dry drawer or cupboard and covered with a cloth if extra protection is needed. In parishes where the church building is heated only during services and linens might become mildewed if left in the damp, linens may be stored elsewhere.

When altar linens wear out, they are customarily not thrown away; instead, they may be burned and the ashes scattered on the earth or washed down the piscina. Of course, linens can be recycled — smaller linens can be made from the undamaged pieces of larger ones.

Checklist for stain removal

1. Red wine — Pour salt on the stain if it is still wet, immerse in cold water, rub the stain out gently, and wash. If the stain is dry, try soaking it in club soda.

2. Lipstick — Apply liquid detergent to the stain and rub gently. Rinse and wash. Another suggestion is to spray the spot with hair spray, rub gently, and then wash.

3. Rust — Wet the stain with lemon juice and gently rub in salt. Dry the linen in the sun and then wash. Or cover the stain with cream of tartar, immerse it in hot water for five minutes, and then wash.

4. Blood — Soak in hydrogen peroxide mixed half and half with ammonia.

5. Scorch mark — If the scorch isn't deep, washing will usually remove the discoloration. If this doesn't work, rub with a cut onion and soak in cold water before washing. If the material is non-washable, soak a cloth in peroxide, lay it over the mark and press with a warm iron.

6. Wax — Remove excess wax by drawing the thumb nail beneath the spot on the other side of the cloth. Soak the spot in varsol. Wash with soap and water. Varsol will remove wax from vestments and hangings. Apply it gently and patiently with a soft, clean cloth. (Varsol appears to be a safe solvent, but it is always wise to test a corner of the fabric for colour-fastness.) Another method for removing wax is to scrape the excess wax off gently with a dull implement such as the back of a knife. Place the spot between two pieces of brown paper bag and iron using the cotton setting. Sponge the stain with alcohol, or lemon and salt, or detergent, and wash.

7. White toothpaste is excellent for all stains. Use a soft toothbrush and rub gently.

8. Soaking polyester in lemon juice is very effective.

9. 1/2 cup (120 mL) white vinegar in the wash acts as a whitener and leaves no odour.

10. 1 cup (230 mL) of club soda mixed with 1 teaspoon (5 mL) of liquid laundry detergent is an all-purpose stain remover.

11. A light touch of masking tape is great for removing soot from fair linens.

Checklist for care of linens
Washing — Treat for stains, soak in cool water if necessary, and wash by hand or gently in the machine using a mild soap. Rinse well.

Ironing — Linens should be slightly damp when they are ironed. The temperature of the iron depends on the fabric. Avoid hot irons on light-weight linens and synthetics. Do not press folds.

Storage — Store flat in drawers or cupboards. Fair linen and credence cloths are rolled onto rollers. Cover with a cloth or acid-free tissue paper if extra protection is needed.

Laundry list

ITEM	NUMBER TAKEN	DATE TAKEN	BY WHOM	DATE RET'D

Vestments

History
The vestments used in the Anglican church today evolved from the street dress of the middle classes of the late Roman period. Woven for the most part from undyed fibres, those garments were off-white or beige. The alb used today as a eucharistic vestment developed from the white Roman tunic, the *tunica alba*. Surplices originated in northern countries in the twelfth century as expanded albs to cover the lined cassocks and fur jackets worn by monks in cold churches. The original name for this vestment was *alba superpelliceum* or alb over the fur. The amice comes from the *amictus*, a neckerchief used to protect other vest-

ments from sweat. The cincture or girdle was the cord or belt girding the tunic. The stole was the scarf used by Roman officials as a sign of rank.

The chasuble evolved from the *casula*, "a little house," or the Roman outer cloak. The cope, dalmatic, and tunicle, like the chasuble, developed from the outdoor cloak commonly worn in the Roman Empire. The maniple, which is seldom used today, comes from the *mappa*, a handkerchief or napkin that Roman consuls would wave as a signal for the games to begin. It was carried in the hand or over the arm because Roman clothes had no pockets. By the fourth century, imperial insignia had been appropriated by local magistrates. When Christianity became the official religion of the empire, a bishop tended to rank socially with a magistrate and was often the same person. Thus bishops acquired the stole, and presbyters acquired it from bishops. Long after these garments had gone out of fashion, they continued to be worn by the clergy. By the fourth and fifth centuries, these vestments were becoming more elaborate, and by the middle ages they were made of expensive cloth, extensively embroidered and decorated. The clerics of the Reformation adopted the cap, hood, and tippet worn by clerics at universities during the late middle ages because they wanted to emphasize that they were more educated than the Roman clergy.

In seventeenth-century Reformation England, the surplice tended to replace the earlier garments. In fact, until the late nineteenth century, the basic vestments of Anglicanism were the surplice for normal use and a black gown for preaching.

The twentieth-century Anglican church has seen a return to the pre-Reformation vestments of the fuller surplice, the longer, more decorated chasuble, the cope, and the stole. Some vestments have been adapted to contemporary fashion, and some are seldom used; in many parishes the hooded alb has replaced the alb and amice, the cassock-alb has com-

Modern cassock/alb

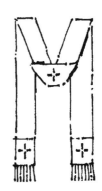

Stole

bined the alb and cassock, and the maniple has been abandoned.

Many liturgical garments are decorated in the traditional style — sometimes because they are inherited, sometimes because people cherish the meanings that have become associated with them. However, in some parishes traditional vestments and hangings are being augmented or replaced by the creations of contemporary liturgical artists.

General vestments

The priest's traditional working garment is the **cassock** — a full-length tunic, long sleeved, high necked, and buttoned down the front or at the side. It may be worn with or without a clerical collar. It is usually black for priests, purple for bishops; but blue, grey, and dark green are sometimes used. The cassock may be worn by choir members and lay assistants. It may be belted with a rope cincture or girdle, a band of material, or a simple leather belt.

For non-eucharistic services, or at the eucharist with a stole, the priest may wear a **surplice** (a white, wide-sleeved garment ideally reaching the ankles) over the cassock. Acolytes, servers, and choir members may wear a surplice or a **cotta** (a shorter version of the surplice) over their cassock.

Either a **stole** (a long, coloured scarf) or a **tippet** (a black scarf used at Morning and Evening Prayer and at burials) is worn around the priest's neck. An **academic hood** may be worn over the cassock and surplice in non-eucharistic offices such as Morning and Evening Prayer, to signify the priest's university degree.

A vestment that is not common in most parishes is the **humeral veil**, a large shawl worn over the shoulders and down the arms of the priest, deacon, or lay person during Solemn Benediction or when the blessed sacrament is carried to the altar of repose on Maundy Thursday. First appearing in the eighth and ninth centuries, this garment was a silk shawl used to cover the hands of the deacon so that he could handle the paten and the gospel book without actually touching them. The **biretta**, a black, square hat with a pompon on the top, and the **Canterbury cap** are seldom worn today.

Eucharistic vestments

Eucharistic vestments are used by the priest, the deacon, and the subdeacon during the celebration of the eucharist. The basic vestment is the **alb**, a long white garment worn over the cassock or on its own. It can be accompanied by an **amice**, a rectangular linen cloth placed over the shoulders, folded down to form a collar, and tied around the waist with long tapes. The amice protects the stole and alb from sweat stains. An **apparel**, a piece of coloured and decorated material, may be attached to the amice and worn as a collar. Apparels may also decorate the sleeves and the hem of the alb. The alb is tied at the waist by a **cincture** or cord belt. The **maniple**, a long band which matches the stole and is looped over the lower arm, is seldom used. The modern cassock-alb, white or off-white, may be worn instead of the alb by either the priest, lay servers, or choir. At the eucharist, the presider may wear the cassock-alb with a stole; the addition of the chasuble is optional.

Amice

Stoles, often coloured according to the day, are worn by both priests and deacons as a sign of their ordination. The stole hangs over both shoulders of the priest and bishop, but over only the left shoulder of the deacon when it is knotted or secured at the right hip. Stoles may be placed either under or over the chasuble. They may be plain or elaborately embroidered or appliquéd.

The **chasuble** is the large, decorated outer garment which may be used by the presider at the eucharist. It is circular or ovoid (like a poncho), although fuller designs may be rectilinear and reach mid-calf. It may be worn during the entire celebration of the eucharist, or from the offertory on. Today the fashion is toward longer, fuller chasubles; they may be very plain or beautifully decorated with traditional or contemporary symbols. Used only in a few parishes, the **dalmatic** and **tunicle** are essentially wide-sleeved over-tunics cut straight at knee length. They are worn by the deacon and subdeacon. Usually the dalmatic has two horizontal bands front and back, while the tunicle has only one. The tunicle may also be worn by the crucifer. The dalmatic was traditionally worn by bishops; when celebrating the eucharist a bishop could wear the chasuble over the episcopal dalmatic. This practice is seldom followed today.

Chasuble

Dalmatic

In procession, on festivals, and other formal occasions, clergy and occasionally lay people may wear a **cope**, a full-length cape, over the alb or surplice. The cope has a **hood** at the back and is held together

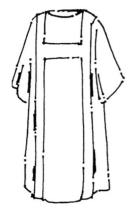

Tunicle

Cope with hood

Bishop in rochet and chimere

at the neck by a large clasp called a **morse**. Traditionally, the cope is made of rich material and may be elaborately decorated with embroidery, fringes, tassels, and braid.

Bishop's vestments

The official dress of Anglican bishops is a purple cassock over which they may wear a **rochet**, a long alb-like vestment with full sleeves gathered at the wrist with a red or black band. Over this they may place a **chimere**, a long black or scarlet gown, sleeveless and open at the front in the fashion of the outdoor coat worn by doctors of divinity in the sixteenth century. Bishops wear a **pectoral cross** around their neck and, as an emblem of their office, an **episcopal ring** on their right hand. The stone in the ring is usually an amethyst, purple being the traditional colour of the episcopate. The **mitre** is a hat signifying the bishop's authority. It may be worn with cope or chasuble at all liturgies, except during prayers. The **crosier**, which the bishop carries in procession, or holds during the reading of the gospel, the absolution, and the blessing, is a staff in the form of a shepherd's crook, symbolizing the bishop's role as pastor of the flock. At the eucharist, the bishop's vesture is the same as a priest's.

Caring for and laying out of vestments

The altar guild looks after vestments, and members with special talents may repair them or even sew new ones.

Vestments made of linen, cotton, or synthetics are laundered and pressed whenever necessary, but they should never be starched. They are placed carefully on hangers to prevent creasing. Chasubles are placed on padded hangers in dust-proof closets or plastic garment bags, or they are laid flat with a minimum of folds and covered with a dust cover in large, custom-made drawers. Maniples, burses, and veils are spread flat in dust-proof drawers. Stoles may also be laid flat in drawers or hung on wide, wooden pegs. Copes are placed on well-padded hangers or dressmaker's dummies and covered, or they may be laid flat in drawers.

If full eucharistic vestments are to be worn during the liturgy, a convenient way to lay them out is first to put out the chasuble, either on a stand or a counter, with the back facing up. The stole is placed on top on one side, the maniple on the other. The cincture is put over them. Over these garments the alb is spread, unbuttoned, with its back facing up. Finally, the amice goes on top with its tapes folded up. This lay-out makes it easy for the celebrant to put on the vestments in the proper order. (See page 71 for chart for laying out vestments.)

Some parishes have fine collections of richly embroidered vestments. Special care must be taken if they are to be cleaned. The textile departments of museums and historical boards may be able to advise on cleaning and preservation.

In time, old vestments will begin to disintegrate and the fabric will need professional restoration. If a garment becomes too worn to be used, the embroidery may be lifted and applied to a new one. Alternatively, the vestment may be retired from use, saved only for display.

Candles

History

The early Christians used candles or lamps of oil to light the table for the eucharistic meal. Candles were incorporated into church ceremony in the fourth century in an order of worship for the evening. Later, they were carried in gospel and buriel processions, given to the newly baptized, placed before the reserved sacrament, and set around the altar (although it was not until the later middle ages that they were put on the altar). From the Reformation to the mid-nineteenth century, lit candles were seldom found on Anglican altars. Today, they are widely used. *The Book of Alternative Services* incorporates the use of candles at the Service of Light at Evening Prayer and for the Great Vigil of Easter. It commends the giving of a candle to the newly baptized, the lighting of the paschal candle during the fifty days between Easter and Pentecost, and the lighting of candles during home prayers. *Occasional Celebrations* explains the lighting of the Advent wreath candles in church and home.

Although lit candles certainly give a festive air and enhance the beauty of the church appointments, their function at a liturgical celebration is not decorative. They call attention to a special time and place of devotion, signify a special action, or give light. When carried in the gospel procession, candles emphasize the honour given to the word of God.

The candles listed here include all those used at the altar or in the church,

Presence lamp

Sanctuary lamp

but it is certainly not essential that a parish use them all. Local custom, the style of the eucharistic celebration, the size and position of the altar, and budget restrictions dictate their use.

Types of candles

The **presence lamp** is a candle, placed in a glass container, which burns continuously before the sacrament when it is reserved in the aumbry or in the tabernacle. Altar workers should check regularly to see if the candle needs replacing. **Sanctuary lamps**, whether one or seven, hang in the sanctuary to dignify the space. These lamps, in glass containers that are usually red, burn independently of the reserved sacrament.

On or behind many altars there are two or more large, permanent **eucharistic** or **altar lights** set in stands high enough so that they can be seen by the congregation but not so large that they overpower the altar. In some parishes, the altar candles are not put on the altar until the offertory and are removed after communion. These candles are usually smaller than those that stay permanently on the altar.

Office lights, six candles of medium height, may be set in stands either on the retable or beside the altar. **Candelabra** (either three, five, or seven branch) are used at special feasts and festivals and are placed on or near the altar. Although it is not common, some churches may have a **bishop's candle** which is put on the altar with the eucharistic candles when the bishop celebrates the eucharist. **Processional torches** are candles in holders set on a staff and carried during the entrance, gospel, and festival processions by torchbearers. When not in use, they are set in stands near the chancel wall. Some churches may have two large candles, **pulpit lights**, set in permanent stands flanking the pulpit or lectern. More common are **pavement candles** set in stands on the floor beside and slightly in front of the corners of the altar. The **paschal candle**, usually decorated with

Christian symbols, is lit at the Great Vigil of Easter and remains in the sanctuary until Pentecost. After that it may stand at the font, and is used during baptisms and at eucharists in commemoration of the departed. Along with the paschal candle, **bier lights** (four or six tall candles set in stands on the floor beside the coffin) may be used at funerals. At baptisms, a **baptismal candle**, lit from the paschal candle, may be given to each of the candidates.

In churches which celebrate the service of Tenebrae during Holy Week, **tenebrae lights** are a part of the service. These lights consist of a triangular stand called a **hearse** holding fifteen candles which are large enough to be seen by the congregation and are ceremonially extinguished during the service. During Advent, some churches light the **candles of the Advent wreath**, one for each of the Sundays before Christmas. These candles may be all white, blue, or purple, or three purple (or blue) and one pink (for Gaudete Sunday, the third Sunday in Advent). Sometimes there is a fifth, white candle in the centre of the wreath, the **Christ candle**.

Candle tubes, also known as everlasting candles, are a practical and economical way of using small ends of candles. The candle stands inside a white or cream-coloured tube and is pressed upwards by a spring; only the burning top of the candle is exposed. However, the candle stub must be long enough to last the service. Canisters of butane may be used instead. The problem with tubes is that the spring may seize and the candle go out, or the butane canister may burn out in mid-service.

In some churches, there may be candle stands in front of pictures and statues. These hold **votive candles**, set in sand in a fireproof container, which are lit by worshippers as an outward sign of prayer.

Care of candles
The candles used for church services are usually made of two-thirds beeswax. Beeswax is a natural material,

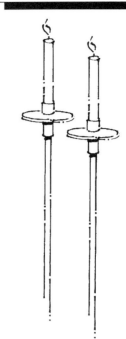

Torches

Paschal candle

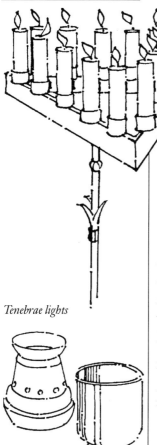

Tenebrae lights

Followers

and candles made of it last longer than those made of paraffin and stearine. When ordering candles, it is important to know both the height and the diameter required.

Candles harden with age and should ideally be stored in a cool place for a couple of months before use. Candles will drip and sputter less if they are kept in the freezer for a day before use. Wax on floors, carpets, or altar linen is a nuisance to remove, so many churches use followers and bobèches to prevent dripping. A **follower** is a chrome, brass, or glass cylindrical top that fits over the candle, preventing drips and prolonging the life of the candle. The sharp edges of the tops of new candles should be bevelled by trimming with a paring knife to a 45-to 60-degree angle. The follower will then fit down on the shaft and prevent the collecting of melted wax which may cause the flame to gutter and smoke or may overflow the follower. A **bobèche** is a flat collar that catches drips of wax; plastic discs are used for large candles, and paper bobèches fit at the base of hand-held tapers.

New candles should be lit for a few minutes before they are used for the first time. The wicks of the lighting taper should be checked and trimmed regularly.

Round or square pieces of plastic may be placed under the foot of candle holders, especially pavement candles, to catch accidental drips during the lighting and extinguishing of candles. There will be fewer drips if those lighting candles are trained to carry the extinguisher or snuffer so that the taper is held upward, turned horizontally when just above the candle, and then turned upward again.

If a candle is somewhat narrow for its holder, a collar of paper can be wrapped around its base. When a candle is slightly too wide for its holder, place the base of the candle in a dish of hot water; the softened wax can be pared away easily. Candles can be made more secure in their holder, by applying the petroleum gum "stick-um" into the base of the holder, or by pouring in hot wax into which the candle settles.

Used candles should be trimmed; the wax is carved away from short wicks, long wicks are cut back to about 1/4 inch (1/2 cm), the tops of the candle are cut flat with a sharp knife, and drips are scraped off the side. Candles themselves may be cleaned either with rubbing alcohol or with salad oil.

Candle holders need to be cleaned of wax before they are stored away or before they are used again. Rinsing in very hot water or pouring hot water over them will remove the hard wax, and rubbing immediately with a cloth or paper towel will wipe away wax residue and polish the surface. The same system is used to clean candle extinguishers and followers. It is wise to use a separate bowl and pour the waxy water outside so as not to clog the drain. A cloth or paper towel soaked in paint thinner will also remove wax residue from holders and followers.

Wax on the floor may be softened with a hair dryer, wiped away with a paper towel, and the spot washed with vinegar and warm water or varsol. Wax on a carpet may be treated first with absorbent paper warmed with an iron, then wiped with cleaning fluid. Lacquered brass is treated the same way as the floor, but rubbed with a soft cloth or paper towel and not washed with vinegar.

Flowers

History
Arrangements of flowers are an almost universal feature in today's churches. However, it was not until the mid-nineteenth century that cut flowers in water were used on or near the altar in Anglican churches. Their use became common only after 1930.

Source of flowers
Flowers may be ordered from the florist; or flowers, greenery, and branches may be collected from the gardens of the congregation. Parishes in rural areas may gather wildflowers and foliage from the fields and woods. Using flowers and greenery from gardens and from the wild not only saves money, since flowers are very expensive in most places in Canada for much of the year, but it also provides some interesting plant material that a florist may not usually stock. Such use also expresses identification with the local environment. However, when collecting flowers and greenery from the wild, it is vital to get the owner's permission, to make sure none of the plants is on the endangered list, and to avoid depleting an area so that no flowers are left to reseed.

Flowers from the gardens of the congregation are a wonderful offering; growing them and giving them to the church is a gift of love. If flowers are bought from the florist, the parish can save money by ordering only a few and supplementing the arrangement with local greens. A parish can encourage a feeling of participation by growing its flowers in a parish garden, looked after by members of the congregation. These flowers enhance both the outside and the inside of the building. Some parishes have potted plants instead of cut flowers, using indoor plants that tolerate lower light levels.

If flowers are bought, they may be contributed by members of the parish, either as a memorial or a thanksgiving. The altar guild or the flower committee may have a secretary who collects the money for these gifts, orders the flowers from the florist, and sees that acknowledgement is made in the bulletin. A flower chart is a convenient way of keeping a record of these gifts, of the type and colour of flowers to be ordered, and to whom they will be given after the service, if that is the custom of the parish. In many churches, it is a tradition for the entire parish to contribute the Christmas and Easter flowers by placing a donation in a special envelope left in the pews a few weeks before these feasts.

The wedding party provides the flowers for weddings, and those on or by the altar normally are left there as a thanksgiving offering. In parishes which regularly receive flowers from a florist, it may be the practice to refer the wedding couple to that florist. Wedding flowers may decorate the chancel, either on stands or on the steps. In some churches, they are not to be placed on the altar; in some, they are, but they must never dominate the altar.

Flowers for funerals are usually provided only by the family and close friends, and the number of arrangements and wreaths in the sanctuary should be limited. If flowers are delivered for the family, they may be placed in the sacristy until after the service. Ideally, there are no flowers on the coffin during the funeral service; the coffin may be covered instead by a pall, symbolizing that all are equally encompassed by God's love in death. If flowers are on the coffin when it arrives for the funeral service, they are placed at the back of the church until the end of the service.

Preparation

The arranging of the flowers may be done by altar guild members who enjoy and have a talent for this, or by those who would like to learn. In some churches, there is a committee whose only task is to arrange the flowers for the various liturgies; in others, the guild members share the responsibility on a rotating basis. If there is no one who can spare the time on Saturday mornings, a florist arranges the flowers.

In planning floral decorations for the church, the first and most important thing to consider is the architecture and size of the building. In large churches and cathedrals, the arrangements are big — with large leaves, flowers, and containers — so that they can be appreciated from a distance. They may be put on pedestals for extra effect. Architecture also dictates the style; the same arrangement would not be appropriate in a simple, colonial-style church and in a Gothic cathedral.

Some churches never have flowers on the altar; others do, except during Lent. Flower arrangements should not distract attention from the altar and from what is going on there. They may enhance, but they must not dominate or in any way overpower the chancel or impede the movements of the presider, the servers, and the people. They must not block the view of any member of the congregation. Flowers are not put in the font, but they may be placed at the foot of the font, and if they are placed near the cross, the cross predominates.

The type and colour of flowers often reflect the nature of the day or season. Certain flowers are traditionally associated with certain seasons: Christmas — poinsettias, holly, ivy, and evergreens; Easter — lilies and other spring flowers. However, when considering the colour, it is important to remember that blue, purple, and lavender tend to recede and even disappear at a distance. Light, strong colours, such as cream, apricot, and pink show best. The background influences floral impact: if the background is dark, lighter flowers work best; if it is light, dark flowers are the most dramatic. Flowers for churches should be bold and large; dainty ones are lovely at close range but will not be seen by the congregation.

When flowers arrive at the church — whether they come from a florist, from members' gardens, or from the wild — they should be cared for immediately. Ideally, the stems are cut again, the lower foliage is stripped off, and the flowers are left to stand in a deep bucket of tepid water for a few hours or overnight before they are arranged. Foliage may be put in the same bucket as the flowers, or it can be kept in

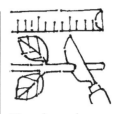

The ends must be cut again, under water, where they remain until the flowers are arranged.

Flowers are left to stand in a deep bucket of tepid water for a few hours or overnight before they are arranged.

Flowers should always be put into a well cleaned vase.

Daffodils can be deadly to other flowers because they secrete a poison into the water. After they have been trimmed, they should stand on their own in water for a whole day; the stems are not cut again when they are put with other flowers. The stamens of tulips and lilies may be snipped off.

another bucket with both the branches and leaves pushed right under water.

Some flowers need special treatment before they are put in water to soak. The stems of gladioli may be cut and placed in hot water for two to three minutes. The stems of roses and other flowers whose heads tend to droop may be dipped into boiling water — one minute for soft stems, and up to five minutes for woody stems. A collar of newspaper around the blossom protects the flower from steam damage. Then the flowers are put overnight into a deep container of cool water. Stripping roses of their foliage and thorns opens up more water-absorbing areas. If carnations droop, a twist tie at the base of the flower will give it additional support. When chrysanthemums begin to loose their petals, a drop of wax applied at the spot will help hold the remaining petals in place. Daffodils can be deadly to other flowers because they secrete a poison into the water. After they have been trimmed, they should stand on their own in water for a whole day; the stems should not be cut again when they are put with other flowers. The stamens of tulips and lilies may be snipped off to prolong the life of the flower and to prevent the pollen from staining furniture, carpets, and linens. Wrapping tulips in a tube of newspaper for the length of the stem and standing them in water overnight will keep them from drooping. But letting them hang over the side of the container will make the stems curve. The cut ends of flowers that have a milky sap in their stems, such as poppies, hollyhocks, dahlias, and poinsettias, should be seared with a match or candle for a second or two to prevent the juice from dripping and the flowers from drooping.

The two causes for wilting flowers are bacteria and air clogging the stems. When a flower is cut, a pocket of air forms at the base of the stem which prevents water from reaching the flower. The end must be cut again, under water, where it remains until the flowers are arranged. If the flower is removed from the water even briefly, another air pocket develops and the stem should be cut again. Stems should never be broken off or flattened, not even woody ones. Bacteria in the water shorten the life of plants; so flowers and greenery must be stored and arranged in scrupulously clean containers. Stripping the leaves below the water line in the final arrangement slows down bacterial growth. It is important to top up the arrangements regularly with clean water, and they should be misted occasionally with water to prevent premature wilting. Cut flowers cannot stand direct sunlight or drafts, and they will last longer if they are removed to a cool place for the night.

Arrangement
Arranging flowers for the church requires time and patience, but it is not so intimidating as it may first seem; with practice most people can learn to do it. Begin with clean containers of a style appropriate to the arrangement.

Chicken wire or a foam block will hold the flowers in place in low vases; in taller vases, crumpled tissue may help hold them upright. Cut the stems with a very sharp knife (preferable to clippers) and place them in a vase or wet oasis immediately. When inserting hollow stemmed flowers into an oasis, the hole should be made in advance with a sharp object such as a pencil, so that foam does not clog the stems. Some flowers such as carnations may need to be wired for extra support. A wire is inserted into the base of the flower, pushed down the stem to above the water line, and wrapped around the stem.

When arranging flowers in their containers, begin with the greenery as a background and then fill in the gaps with the flowers, or begin with the flowers and fill in the spaces with greens. Placing the stems so that they seem to radiate from a central point creates a more graceful effect. Arranging the flowers so that the larger ones are in the centre facing forward, while the smaller ones turn away from the centre, creates a feeling of depth. Lighter coloured flowers should be placed towards the outside of the arrangement, darker ones inside. The traditional shape for most church arrangements is the triangle, with the flowers one-and-a-half times the height of the vase, or the round arrangement, one-and-a-half times the width of the vase.

Flower arranging

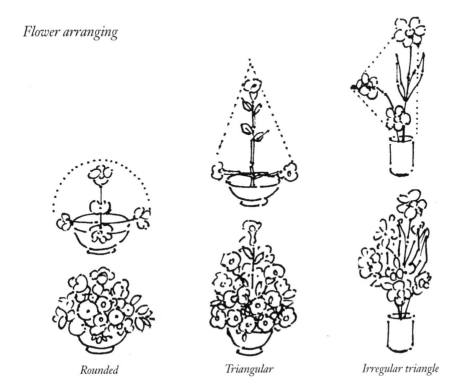

Rounded   Triangular   Irregular triangle

In many churches, altar flowers are delivered to the sick or shut-in after the service. Large, plastic glasses or containers can be used as temporary containers to hold and transport these gifts. Often a note or card mentioning that the flowers are accompanied by the prayers of the congregation is included.

Flower chart

DATE	FEAST OF	CONTRIB. BY	ARRANGED BY	IN MEMORY OF	DISPOSITION TO	BY
——	————	————	————	————	———	————
——	————	————	————	————	———	————
——	————	————	————	————	———	————
——	————	————	————	————	———	————
——	————	————	————	————	———	————
——	————	————	————	————	———	————
——	————	————	————	————	———	————
——	————	————	————	————	———	————
——	————	————	————	————	———	————

Services: the setting up

The first two sections of this book describe the use, history, and care of the appointments of the church — the building, furniture, vessels, linens, vestments, candles, and flowers. This section will suggest how altar workers may set up these appointments for regular as well as less common services. The instructions will be general and for many too extensive. Every parish has its own way of celebrating its liturgies depending on its tradition, the preference of the incumbent, the decisions of the worship committee, the architecture of the building, and the appointments available. Consequently, the checklists are only guidelines. They should be edited and amended by the persons responsible for the conduct of the liturgy in each parish.

The Book of Alternative Services and The Book of Common Prayer contain liturgies for the sacramental rites, holy days, and other offices; other liturgies are included in Occasional Celebrations. These are the services for which altar workers prepare.

The eucharist

The eucharist is the liturgy most often celebrated in Anglican parishes, usually on Sundays, often more than once, and sometimes during the week. Many of the church's other rites take place within the context of a eucharist.

The Holy Eucharist is the principal act of Christian worship; it is the gathering of the community, the Body of Christ. With baptism, it is the earliest

Christian liturgical celebration. After the death of Jesus, his disciples continued to meet in the Jewish tradition of communal meals, to remember their master who had shared food with them the night before his crucifixion. And when they did, they found he was still with them. The custom of the meal continued, first in private homes, then, as the Christian community grew, in larger meeting places. The contemporary liturgical movement is restoring some of the elements of early Christian practice.

In some celebrations today, after the Gathering of the Community and the Proclamation of the Word, the worshippers meet around an altar or table, covered with a white cloth. They bring the bread and wine to the celebrant, and they may distribute communion to one another. Preparation for this type of celebration takes relatively little time. Elsewhere, the eucharistic feast may be far more elaborate: many vessels are used, the priests, deacons, and other ministers are fully vested, the church is decorated, incense and bells may be part of the ceremony, and a procession may take place. Preparing for this type of service is more detailed and time-consuming.

Preparation
As for any feast, celebration, or special family dinner, the house must be got in order. In some parishes, the altar guild is responsible for cleaning the church, for dusting and sweeping; in others, the sexton or caretaker does this work, perhaps with the help of professional cleaning people, and the guild members are responsible only for the sanctuary and the sacristy. In some churches, the guild lays out the leaflets, prayer books and hymnals; in others, this is the ushers' or sidesmen's task.

Most of the preparation for a Sunday eucharist usually takes place the day before. Beginning with the chancel, altar workers dust and occasionally polish the furniture, sweep the floor, remove candle wax from the carpet, and vacuum it. They replace the fair linen and the credence cloth, if necessary; change the frontal and frontlet, the falls and markers for the season or the occasion; and remove the dust cover, although that may be done by the servers just before the Sunday service. The sanctuary candles are checked, the wicks trimmed, the drips scraped, and the followers and bobèches cleaned. The candle holders for the eucharistic lights, the office lights, and the pavement lights are buffed and occasionally polished. The kneeling cushions are straightened, and if the backs of the benches in the sanctuary are to be covered, the sedilia cloths are hung.

Continuing in the sacristy, the altar workers remove old wax from the candle snuffers and polish them. The wicks are trimmed and checked for easy movement in the tube. Altar guild members clean and polish the processional cross, the torches, the collection plates, and the alms basin. Banners, mounted on their poles, are put out, ready for the procession. The candles are trimmed, and their holders are cleaned of wax and buffed or polished. The candelabra are set up if they are to be used. The altar book and its stand are put in the appropriate place — the altar, the credence table (if there is space) or on another table. If a Bible is used for the readings, it is put in its place. These books may have coloured markers, matching the colour of the day, to indicate the beginning of the service, the propers, and the readings. The books are usually left closed. The alms basin is placed on or under the credence table or in a suitable niche. The collection plates are put in their place. In some parishes, because of the danger of theft, many of these articles may be set out in the sacristy, ready to be placed in the sanctuary before the service.

Preparation of the eucharistic vessels may vary according to local custom and the type of celebration, and can depend on the size of the congregation, when and how the elements are brought to the altar, the type of bread that is used, and whether or not the chalice is vested. To begin with, all the vessels are cleaned. Regular washing in soapy water, rinsing in clear water, and a good rub are generally enough to keep silver shiny. Care should be taken not to immerse the bases of the vessels in water, because water will get trapped in the cracks and seams and later leak onto the cloths.

The chalice is vested according to the custom of the parish. In some parishes, a purificator is draped over the chalice, a paten with a priest's host on top is next, then a chalice pall and a veil, and finally a burse which contains the corporal and an extra purificator (see the chart on page 68). There are two ways of hanging the veil; it may cover all sides of the chalice evenly with the embroidered decoration facing the congregation, or the veil may cover only three sides of the chalice with the fourth side folded over the top. The burse is laid with the open side usually on

Chalice

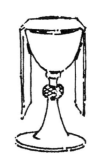

Chalice with purificator

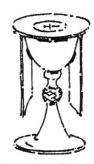

Chalice with purificator, paten, and host

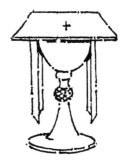

Chalice with purificator, paten, host, and pall

Vesting a chalice

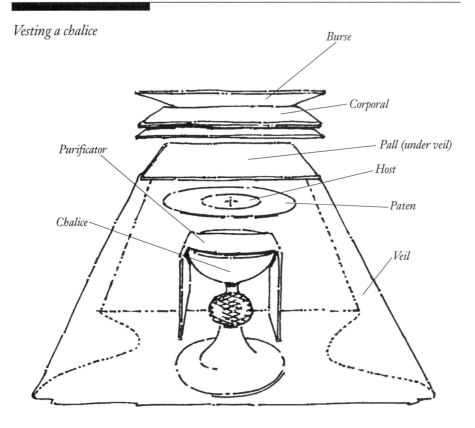

Chalice with purificator, paten, host, and pall covered with veil and topped with burse containing the corporal

Placement of vessels

Here is one way of setting out the vessels

the right or else facing the priest. It and the veil customarily match the colour of the day. If more than one chalice will be used, the others are vested with a purificator and possibly a chalice pall, ready to be placed on the credence table. The wine flagon or cruets are filled, but not right to the top. The lavabo bowl, towel, and cruet of water are set out on a tray, with any handles facing out.

Some parishes place the vested chalice on the altar before the eucharist. The bread box or ciborium and the flagon or cruet of wine are placed on the credence table near the altar in the sanctuary. If wafers are used, altar workers should estimate how many will be needed and place them in the ciborium or breadbox. For the priest's information it is helpful to include a small piece of paper in the vessel indicating the number of wafers.

Other parishes follow the "low mass" custom, adopted by some Anglicans in the nineteenth century, of having the celebrant carry the veiled chalice to the altar. Today, many parishes and their priests, realizing the symbolic significance of leaving the table bare until after the Proclamation of the Word, transfer the chalice to the altar from the credence table only during the Preparation of the Gifts. Alternatively, representatives of the people may carry the chalice, the bread, and the wine to the altar in an offertory procession reminiscent of early Christian ceremonies. In this case, the bread, a flagon or cruet of wine, and sometimes the empty chalice are set on a small table in the nave of the church where the people can see their offering. A white cloth may cover this table and a lighted candle may be placed on it, to be extinguished when the offering is brought to the altar. Some parishes encourage the people to take a wafer from a breadbox and place it into a ciborium or a dish as they enter the church.

Extra chalices for the chalice bearers, extra bowls or plates for the distribution of bread, and extra purificators and corporals may be set out on the credence table. In many parishes, the final setting up of these vessels and linens takes place just before the eucharist and is done either by altar guild members or by the acolytes and servers. Until that time, the vessels are kept in the sacristy on a sacristy credence table or a shelf.

The flowers are arranged the day before the service and placed either on the retable or on stands, or are kept in the sacristy until just before the service. If incense will be a part of the celebration, the thurible is cleaned; and the boat, the incense, the spoon, and matches are set out in the sacristy, preferably on a fireproof surface. The sanctus bells, if used, may be placed near the altar on the epistle side or under the credence table.

The last preparation for the eucharist is the laying out of the vestments for the day. This may be quite simple or more time-consuming and complex, depending on the number and the order of the ministers involved. The vestments for the ministers are laid out on a vesting table or on clothes stands in reverse

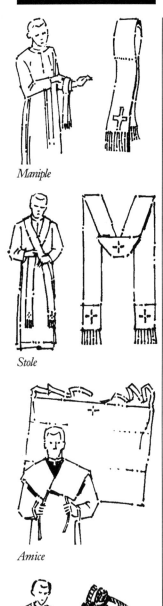

Maniple

Stole

Amice

Cincture

order to that in which they are put on — chasuble first (front side facing down), maniple, stole, cincture, alb, and finally the amice (if all of these are used). They may be covered with a dust cloth. (See the chart on page 71.) The servers and the acolytes usually get their own vestments ready.

Finally, the sacristy is put in order, the floors swept, the counters cleaned, and the sinks washed. All this preparation is made easier if charts and diagrams showing the parish's ways of vesting vessels and placing them on a table ready for the service, and of laying out the priest's vestments, are posted in the sacristy. A checklist of preparatory work will remind altar workers of the things that need to be done (see page 72).

Any final preparations on the day of the eucharist should be done as unobtrusively as possible. It is very distracting for people coming into the church to see altar workers hurrying about the altar in a last-minute frenzy. Arriving at the church early allows workers plenty of time to look after any final details.

After the service

After the eucharist, when the candles have been snuffed out and the congregation has dispersed, altar workers may begin the work of putting away and tidying up. Basically this is a reverse of the preparation. All the vessels, as well as the altar book and extra candles, are carried back into the sacristy. Any extra consecrated bread and wine are stored separately, usually in the tabernacle. Any leftover, unconsecrated wine is poured back into its bottle, and unconsecrated wafers are wrapped up for further use. The chalices and patens are rinsed with boiling water, and the water may be poured down the piscina (or on the ground). Then the vessels are thoroughly washed in warm, soapy water, rinsed, dried with a soft cloth used for no other purpose, and stored away in a safe place. The purificators and the corporal are rinsed, and the water may be poured

Laying out of vestments

The vestments for the ministers are laid out on a vesting table or on clothes stands in reverse order to that in which they are put on - chasuble first (front side facing down) followed by the maniple, stole, cincture, alb, and amice.

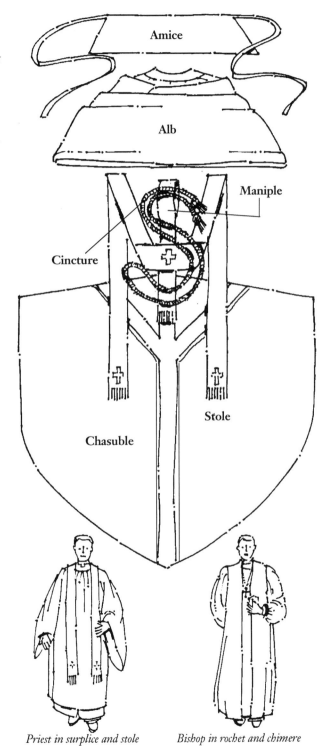

Amice

Alb

Maniple

Cincture

Stole

Chasuble

Priest vested for the eucharist

Deacon in surplice and stole

Priest in surplice and stole

Bishop in rochet and chimere

down the piscina. Stained linen should be treated or soaked as soon as possible. The linen to be laundered is stored in a special place, ready to be taken home by the laundry team. Other linens are returned to their place, and the fair linen on the altar is covered with a protector. If incense has been used, the thurible may be soaked so that it can be cleaned easily later on. The eucharistic vestments are put back in their drawers. Everything is returned to its assigned place and the sanctuary and the sacristy are left clean and tidy.

Checklist for the eucharist
This sample list can be added to or subtracted from, and can be the basis for each altar guild's own check list of work to be done before and after the eucharist.

Before the Eucharist

In the Sanctuary
- Dust, sweep, and vacuum the chancel. Polish any furniture that may need it.
- Change fair linen and credence cloth, if necessary. Change frontal and frontlet, falls and markers, according to the season.
- Check candles, trim wicks, scrape drips, clean followers and bobèches.
- Remove wax from candle holders and polish, if necessary.
- Straighten kneeling cushions and put out sedilia cloths.

In the sacristy
- Polish and trim candle snuffers. Polish processional cross, torches, collection plates, and alms basin. Put out banners.
- Trim candles, polish holders, and set up candelabra.
- Put out altar book and stand and Bible.
- Put out alms basin and collection plates.
- Clean vessels.
- Vest chalice.
- Fill flagon and cruets.
- Put out bread or wafers.
- Put out lavabo bowl and towels.
- Arrange flowers.
- Set out the cleaned thurible, incense, boat, spoon, and matches.
- Set out sanctus bells.
- Lay out vestments.
- Tidy sacristy.

After the Eucharist
- Take vessels, altar book, and extra candles back to the sacristy.
- Store leftover consecrated bread and wine separately. Pour unconsecrated wine back into the bottle and wrap up unconsecrated wafers.
- Rinse chalices and patens with boiling water. Wash with warm, soapy water, dry, and store.
- Rinse purificators and corporals and treat them for stains as soon as possible.
- Cover fair linen on altar.
- Soak thurible.
- Put back eucharistic vestments.
- Tidy sacristy.

Baptism

The sacrament of Holy Baptism marks the beginning of new life in Christ. In the early days of Christianity, initiation into the church was the concern of the entire community. Baptisms took place in the midst of the people in the context of a eucharist, during the all-night vigil that preceded the Easter dawn. Today's church has reintroduced that practice, and there is a new stress on the presence of the congregation; private baptism takes place less frequently. *The Book of Common Prayer* (page 522) recommends that the service occur on Sundays or holy days in the presence of the congregation; *The Book of Alternative Services* strongly encourages it (pages 146–147).

Apart from the regular setting up for the major Sunday eucharist, altar guild members have a few extra responsibilities when there is a baptism. Preparation begins at the font. The cover is removed, and the font is dusted. The paschal candle is checked, drips are scraped off, and the wick is trimmed for easy lighting. Matches should be put out in a safe and convenient place. Prayer or service books, with the appropriate page marked, may be laid out near the font for the baptismal party.

In the sacristy, items for the baptism are set out, to be carried into the church before the service. A large pitcher or ewer will carry water to the font. A baptismal shell may be used to pour water over the baptismal candidate's head, and a towel will be used for drying. Each candidate may be given a baptismal candle to symbolize new life. In parishes where candidates are anointed with chrism, a stock of holy oil is set out. Before the service, an altar guild member can fill the pitcher with lukewarm water and pour it into the font, bring out the other baptismal items, and place them nearby on a credence table or on the edge of the font.

After the service, the baptismal accoutrements are returned to their place;

Baptismal shell

water from the font, if it does not have a drain going directly into the earth, is removed (it may be poured into the piscina or onto the ground); the font is wiped dry; and the cover is replaced. The baptismal towel may not need laundering but may be spread out to dry before being returned to its drawer.

Checklist for baptism
Before the service
- Complete usual preparation for the eucharist.
- Dust the font and remove the cover.
  Trim the paschal candle and put out matches if they will be needed.
- Lay out service books near the font for the baptismal party.
- Set out a large pitcher or ewer, baptismal shell, and towels.
- Put out baptismal candles and a stock of holy oil.
- Just before the service, fill the jug with lukewarm water and pour it into the font.

After the service
- Return baptismal accoutrements to their place. Make sure the baptismal towels are dry before putting them away.
- Remove water from the font, dry it, and replace the cover.

Divine offices

In some parishes, Morning Prayer (Mattins) may still be the principal liturgical act on a Sunday. Morning Prayer as Sunday worship dates from the sixteenth century. *The Book of Common Prayer* and *The Book of Alternative Services* offer liturgies for both Morning and Evening Prayer and also for mid-day. The liturgical developments of the last twenty years have restored the eucharist as the central service for many congregations, and Morning Prayer, as the principal Sunday service, is becoming less common. Evening

Prayer is being sung or said less frequently in most parishes. *The Book of Alternative Services* offers an optional office for use on Saturday night — the Saturday Vigil of the Resurrection — a revival of a fourth-century, weekly vigil welcoming Sunday as the Lord's Day.

Preparation for these offices begins with the same cleaning, tidying, and checking of the church and the sanctuary as for the eucharist. For Morning Prayer, the dust cover may remain on the fair linen, or another cover may be used. The frontal, frontlet, falls, and markers are changed according to the season. The candles and candle holders are made ready; the alms basin and plates, the candle snuffers and torches are polished and put in their places. Flowers may or may not be used, depending on the season, and the eucharistic candles are either removed from the altar or not lit. In most cases, the vestments are cassock, surplice, hood, and tippet. Normally, altar workers are not expected to set these out for the officiant.

Solemn Evensong, sung or celebrated with the use of incense, is appropriate on Saturdays, Sundays, and feast days. The vestments for the officiant are cassock and surplice (or cassock-alb and stole) with a cope. If there are assisting deacons, they wear vestments appropriate to their order. The altar guild sets out the processional cross and two torches to precede the officiant into the sanctuary. The thurible, incense boat, and spoon may be used as well.

The Saturday Vigil of the Resurrection begins with the Service of Light during which the ministers may carry one or more candles, and incense may be used. At the prayer of Thanksgiving for Water, the congregation may gather around the font or a container of water.

Checklist for Morning and Evening Prayer
Before the service
- Clean, tidy, and check the church as before a eucharist.
- Check the altar linen. Remove dust cover, if that is the custom.
- Change frontal and frontlet, falls and markers according to the season.
- Prepare candles, clean holders, snuffers, alms basin, offertory plates, and torches.
- Arrange and set out flowers.
- Lay out the vestments, if that is the custom.
- For Solemn Evensong, set out thurible, incense, boat, spoon, and matches.
- Set out processional cross and torches.
- Set out a container of water, if it is to be used at the Prayer of Thanksgiving for Water.

After the service
- Return the dust cover to the altar.
- Return accoutrements to their place in the sacristy.
- Soak the thurible after Solemn Evensong.
- Tidy up the sacristy.

Pastoral and episcopal offices

These offices occur only occasionally; however, altar workers should be aware of the preparations that may be needed. Some of these rites may take place in the context of the eucharist, and the basic elements of the housekeeping remain the same. The altar guild should consult the priest for specific instructions.

Marriage
The Book of Alternative Services notes that "where both bride and groom are entitled to receive communion, it is desirable that the form of service in which the marriage rite is incorporated into the celebration of the eucharist be used" (page 527). In this case, the wedding ceremony is woven into the eucharistic rite, and preparation includes regular housekeeping for the eucharist. However, altar workers may be asked to look after some of the other details of the ceremony.

Even if the flowers have been arranged by a florist, altar guild members are responsible for placing them in the chancel. Flowers in the chancel should be arranged in the church's containers; other floral arrangements may be placed in the narthex or the nave. Flowers at or on the altar are normally left as a thank offering by the wedding party. The altar guild prepares the altar candles as well as any others that may be used. Kneelers or wedding cushions are placed in the centre of the sanctuary. The marriage register and a pen are set out on a table in the sanctuary, unless the signing is to take place in the vestry. If holy water is used, the aspergillium and asperges bucket are brought out; if there is to be incense, the thurible is prepared.

When there is no eucharist and the service for the Celebration and Blessing of a Marriage is used, the setting up is similar except that eucharistic preparations are not made. The vestments may be surplice and stole or alb and stole, with or without a cope.

Checklist for marriage
Before the service
- Regular eucharistic preparation if the ceremony is to take place within the context of a eucharist.

- Position the flowers.
- Prepare candles and candelabra.
- Set out kneelers or wedding cushions.
- Set out marriage register and pen on a table in the sanctuary or in the vestry.
- Bring out asperges bucket and aspergillium.
- Set out thurible, incense, boat, spoon, and matches.
- Lay out vestments, if necessary.

After the service
- Regular post-eucharistic cleanup, if a eucharist has been celebrated.
- Flowers in the chancel remain, other flowers may be returned to the wedding party.
- Return candelabra, wedding cushions, marriage register, pen, asperges bucket, and aspergillium to the sacristy.
- Soak the thurible.
- Leave the sacristy clean and tidy.

The funeral liturgy
Again, preparation depends on whether or not a eucharist will be part of the liturgy. Although black vestments have been used traditionally for funeral eucharists, white vestments are being used more frequently. If there is no eucharist, altar workers will vest the altar and lay out a surplice, stole, and cope for the priest. The placement of any flowers in the sanctuary should be checked. The funeral pall, which may need to be ironed, is placed at the door, ready to cover the coffin as it is carried into the church; there usually are no flowers on the coffin during the service. If they are to be used, the office lights and the bier candles on either side of the casket will be lit. The asperges bucket is filled with holy water and the thurible is prepared, if these are to be used.

   If a eucharist is to be celebrated, preparations are made for that as well: eucharistic vestments are laid out, the chalice is vested, and the eucharistic candles are prepared.

Checklist for funerals
Before the service
- Regular eucharistic preparations if a eucharist is to be celebrated.
- Check placement of flowers.
- Place the funeral pall near the entrance.
- Set out office lights, bier candles, processional cross, and torches.
- Prepare asperges bucket and aspergillium.
- Set out thurible, incense, boat, spoon, and matches.

• Lay out vestments, if necessary.

After the service
• Regular eucharistic cleanup if the eucharist has been celebrated.
• Return items to their place.
• Leave the sacristy clean and tidy.

Confirmation
The rite of confirmation is being re-examined within the Anglican Communion. Confirmation, reception, and the reaffirmation of baptismal vows are usually administered at the same time as baptism, in the context of a eucharist. The bishop's chair is placed in the middle of the chancel, the bishop's candle may be set out, and a cushion for those kneeling to be confirmed may be placed in front of the chair. Bishops usually bring their own vestments, equipment, and holy oil; and the bishop's chaplain, not the altar guild, is responsible for their set-up.

Checklist for confirmation
• Same preparation and tidy up as for the eucharist.
• Set up the bishop's chair and candle.
• Put out kneeling cushion for the candidates.

Ordination
The ordination of bishops, priests, and deacons usually takes place on Sundays or other feasts. Here, too, the bishop presides. The context is always the eucharist which is the climax of the rite. Altar guild responsibilities include the regular eucharistic preparations, setting out extra vestments, and putting out a Bible for each ordinand. (*The Book of Alternative Services* requires a Bible, a chalice, and a paten for each new priest.) The bishop's chair is placed in the sanctuary, and a white candle may be placed on the altar to honour the bishop's presence.

Checklist for ordination
• Same preparation and tidy up as for the eucharist.
• Lay out any extra vestments.
• Prepare bishop's chair and candle.
• Put out a Bible for each ordinand.

Liturgies for holy days

The holy days which may require special preparation are Ash Wednesday, the Sunday of the Passion, Maundy Thursday, Good Friday, and the Great Vigil of

Easter. Customs for the celebration of these days vary greatly from church to church, and guild members should consult their priest concerning special directions.

Ash Wednesday

The Ash Wednesday liturgy in *The Book of Alternative Services* includes the imposition of ashes on the forehead with the words, "Remember that you are dust, and to dust you shall return." The ashes come from the burning of the left-over palms of the previous year's Palm Sunday. This preparation may be the responsibility of the altar guild. The dried palms are burnt carefully in a fireproof container; the cooled ashes are sieved to break down the larger pieces, and ground into a fine powder with mortar and pestle. A small amount of ash goes a long way, so it is not necessary to burn large quantities of palms. The ashes may be stored in a pill container.

For the Ash Wednesday liturgy, altar workers should make sure that there is a dish of ashes on the credence table, and that a lavabo bowl and extra towels are provided. Because ash stain may be difficult to remove, some parishes use disposable towels for wiping the priest's hands. If the ashes are to be blessed, the asperges bucket (containing holy water) and aspergillium may be set out. If the ashes are to be censed, the thurible is prepared. If some ash falls on a piece of linen, the ash should be shaken off, and the spot blotted with cold water and a soft cloth. Further laundering may not be necessary. Do not rub the fabric, as this may set the stain further.

Checklist for Ash Wednesday
• Same preparation and tidy up as for the eucharist.
• Prepare ashes and set them out on the credence table.
• Make sure a lavabo bowl and extra towels are provided.
• Set out the asperges bucket and aspergillium.
• Prepare the thurible.

The Sunday of the Passion

The rites of Holy Week are very different from those of the rest of the church year. They begin with the Sunday of the Passion (Palm Sunday), include Maundy Thursday and Good Friday, and end with the Great Vigil of Easter. Consultation is required among the altar guild, the priest, and the worship committee because the liturgy in *The Book of Alternative Services* may be new to some people.

The liturgy of the Sunday of the Passion begins with pomp and glory, the hosannas of Jesus' triumphal entry into Jerusalem; but with the reading of the

Asoperges bucket and aspergilllium

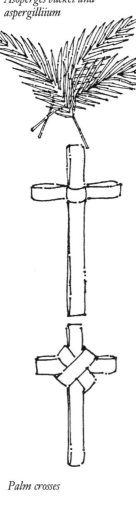

Palm crosses

Passion, the tone changes to "Crucify him, crucify him." The rites begin with the liturgy of the palms and, possibly, the entire congregation processing into and through the church. Before the service, palm fronds are distributed to the people who, ideally, have gathered in a place outside the church, the parish hall, for example. In some churches, branches other than palms are used (for example, pussy willows); however, in most of Canada the trees are still bare at this time of the year.

Special duties for the day, other than the regular eucharistic ones, include ordering palms well in advance and setting them out in baskets on a table covered with a credence cloth. If holy water is used, the aspergillium and asperges bucket are put nearby; if incense is part of the celebration, the thurible is prepared. The sanctuary may be decorated with vases of palm fronds, and palm fronds may be attached to the processional cross. The colour of the day is passiontide red, so the frontal and hangings are changed. The celebrant may wear a cope for the liturgy of the palms and change into a chasuble for the eucharist.

Checklist for the Sunday of the Passion
• Same preparation and tidy up as for the eucharist.
• Set out the palm fronds in a basket on a credence table.
• Set out aspergillium and asperges bucket.
• Prepare thurible.
• Palm fronds may be attached to the processional cross.

Maundy Thursday
The Maundy (from *mandatum novum* — a new commandment, John 13:34) Thursday liturgy, which is celebrated in the evening, provides for the ceremony of the washing of feet and the stripping of the altar at the end of the eucharist. This is a solemn celebration, a thanksgiving for the institution of the

eucharist, and the beginning of the sacred three days commemorating the passion, death, and resurrection of our Lord.

The frontal, the hangings, and the vestments are white or red. Special preparation may include the provision of a basin, a pitcher of water, a cloth, and towels for the ceremony of the washing of the feet which commemorates Jesus' washing of his disciples' feet at the Last Supper and symbolizes self-giving. The furniture in the sanctuary may need to be re-arranged or extra chairs brought into the chancel.

If the stripping of the altar includes washing it, materials for washing the altar are set out; in some churches, the tradition is to wash the altar with wine or wine and water. In some parishes, altar workers help the priest with the stripping of the altar, carrying the candles, vessels, linen, and flowers back into the sacristy. Crosses that cannot be removed may be veiled.

At the end of the liturgy, it may be the custom to move the sacrament to an altar of repose, a chapel altar or an altar in another room, where it will remain until the Good Friday liturgy. If so, the humeral veil may be set out for the procession to that altar. At the altar of repose, a corporal is placed on the table, a white cloth is set out to completely cover the vessels containing the sacrament, and a presence lamp or vigil candle is made ready. Other candles and candelabra may be used. When the reserved sacrament is brought there before the final stripping of the altar, the elements will be completely veiled, and a vigil candle will be lit. A prayer watch may be kept throughout the night or until midnight by members of the congregation. The altar guild may be responsible for preparing all the details for the altar of repose.

Checklist for Maundy Thursday
- Same preparation and tidy up as for the eucharist.
- Prepare a basin, pitcher of water, and towels for the ceremony of the washing of the feet.
- Set out extra chairs for the ceremony of the washing of the feet.

The foot washing

- Prepare materials for washing the altar.
- Set out veils for crosses and statues.
- Put out the humeral veil.
- Prepare the altar of repose.
- Prepare the presence lamp and extra candles and candelabra.

Good Friday

The Book of Alternative Services provides a moving liturgy to celebrate our Lord's Passion, and many churches today have replaced the three hours' devotion with this rite. It includes the Meditation on the Cross, a tradition which dates to the early days of the church in Jerusalem. A wooden cross is brought into the church between two torches or candles and is set up in a place where all the congregation can see it. There may or may not be a eucharist, and the reserved sacrament from Maundy Thursday may be distributed.

The altar guild is responsible for putting out whatever linen may be necessary: corporal, chalice purificators, and perhaps the fair linen for the altar. Chalices for the administration of communion are got ready. The lavabo bowl, towel, and a cruet of water for the ablutions may also be set out.

The altar will be bare at the beginning of the liturgy, without vestings, candles, or cross. For the meditation on the cross, a wooden cross may be brought into the sacristy, ready to be carried out into the sanctuary after the intercessions, preceded by acolytes carrying candles. A stand for the cross and candle holders for the candles are to be ready to place on or before the altar at this time. The altar book and its stand, a Bible or the lectionary texts, and texts for the participants in the reading of the Passion should be available.

The colour of the day is passiontide red. Some priests may wear full eucharistic vestments; others, seeking greater simplicity, may wish to celebrate the liturgy in alb and red stole; others may wear the alb and stole only after the veneration of the cross.

Checklist for Good Friday
- The eucharist may or may not be celebrated.
- The altar remains bare until after the hymn following the Meditation on the Cross and the anthems.
- Set out a wooden cross and its stand in the sacristy.
- Get candles and torches ready.
- Lay out fair linen and other linens.
- Set out altar book with stand, Bible or lectionary texts, and texts for readers.
- Set out lavabo bowl, cruet of water, and towel.
- Lay out vestments.

The Great Vigil of Easter

There is no celebration of the eucharist on Holy Saturday; the altar remains stripped, and only the wooden cross is on the altar. A simple liturgy of the word may take place.

However, this is a day of much work for the altar guild because, after a brief Holy Saturday liturgy, the preparation for the Great Vigil begins. This celebration is the culmination of the rites of Holy Week, the celebration of our redemption, the commemoration of Christ's resurrection. *The Book of Alternative Services* has restored this service as the apex of the church year, and its rites are wonderfully symbolic. The ceremony begins in darkness and moves to stunning brightness; it begins in silence and proceeds to joyous alleluias; it moves solemnly through the story of our passover from death to life.

The kindling of the new fire and the lighting of the paschal candle, outside or in the back of the church, require the following: for the fire — a fireproof basin (a wok or a Hibachi are good), charcoal or kindling, matches or a lighter, a pocket flashlight, and a fire extinguisher in case of emergency; for the paschal candle — the candle, stylus if the candle is to be inscribed, grains of incense if they are put into the candle, and a taper to light the candle. Candles should be placed in the narthex ready for distribution to the people when they arrive.

If there are to be baptisms, the font is prepared, and the baptismal shell, a pitcher of water, towels, the oil, and the baptismal candles are placed nearby (see page 74 for baptismal preparation). If there are to be confirmations, preparations for the bishop's participation are made (see page 78 for preparation for confirmation). If the people are to be sprinkled with holy water after the renewal of vows, this is done with water from the font, using an aspergillium or a sprig of pine or spruce.

In the chancel, a stand for the paschal candle and a lectern with a reading light for the Exsultet text are

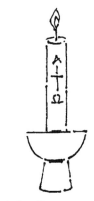

Paschal candle

set out. A Bible or the lections are ready on the lectern for the liturgy of the word. The shrouds are removed. The frontal and hangings are white, as are the vestments. Extra candelabra may be used. The Easter flowers are prepared and brought out into the chancel. The rest of the preparations are as for Sunday eucharists except that more bread and wine may be needed because of the probability of a larger number of communicants.

Checklist for the Great Vigil
• Same preparation and tidy up as for the eucharist.
• The colour of the day is white.
• For the fire, set out a fireproof basin, kindling, matches or lighter, a pocket flashlight, and a fire extinguisher.
• For the paschal candle, set out the candle, a stylus, grains of incense, and a taper. Set out the candle stand in the sanctuary.
• Place candles for the congregation in the narthex.
• If there are to be baptisms, prepare the font. Set out a pitcher of water, the baptismal shell, towels, oil, and baptismal candles.
• If there are to be confirmations, prepare the bishop's chair and candle and a kneeling cushion.
• Put out the aspergillium and the asperges bucket.
• Set out a lectern with a reading light for the Exsultet.
• Prepare extra candelabra and the thurible.

Occasional Services

Occasional Celebrations supplies liturgies for events and occasions in the life of the church and of individuals when people want to pray together. It is a supplement to *The Book of Alternative Services*; none of the rites are mandatory nor need they be followed absolutely. They "should be regarded as models and not as rigid scripts....These texts should be used as the basis of adaptation which evokes the liturgical creativity of the local church" (*Occasional Celebrations*, page 7). It is advisable that there be a meeting of the priest, a representative of the altar guild, musicians, acolytes, and lay assistants before the service to arrange the details.

Appendices

Appendix 1

Service of initiation

All Christians are commissioned for ministry at their baptism and no further form of commissioning is necessary for lay ministry. Individuals who undertake a particular ministry share in the task of equipping "the saints for the work of ministry, for building up the Body of Christ" (Eph 4.12). The form which follows is intended for use when public recognition of a particular lay ministry is desired. It may be used at the beginning of a professional ministry, for example, of a youth worker or a parish musician, or to recognize volunteer ministers such as wardens, members of the parish council or vestry, Sunday school teachers, choristers, members of the altar guild, pastoral visitors, and acolytes or servers. It may also be used when a member of the parish assumes a ministry in the community on behalf of the parish.

A number of people may be commissioned to related ministries at the same time, but the distinctive features of different ministries should be clear in the celebration of the rite.

Following the sermon (and creed) at the eucharist, or before the Intercessions and Thanksgivings at morning or evening prayer, those to be commissioned stand before the presiding minister.

Commissioning for lay ministries in the Church

The presiding minister says in these or similar words.
Brothers and sisters in Christ, we are all baptized by the one Spirit into one body, and given gifts for a variety of ministries for the common good.

Our purpose today is to recognize and affirm the *ministry* for which *this person* has offered *himself/herself*.

The presiding minister describes the ministry and then continues

Is it your will that *N* (*or NN*) fulfil this ministry?
People   **It is.**
The presiding minister addresses those to be commissioned.
N (or *NN*), you have been called to this ministry. Will you, as long as you are engaged in this work, perform it with care, to the honour of God and the benefit of the Church?
Answer   **I will.**

The presiding minister addresses the congregation.
Let us pray.
Blessed are you, gracious God,
our creator and redeemer.
In every age you call people
to minister in your name.
May the work of *this* your *servant*
so build up your Church,
that we may faithfully serve you
and show your love in all the world.
Blessed are you, O God,
now and for ever.
    Amen.

Symbols appropriate to the ministry may be presented. The presiding minister may say,
N (*or NN*), the Lord enable and uphold you in this ministry.

The service continues with the Prayers of the People, or the Intercessions and Thanksgivings, during which prayers may be offered for the ministry of the congregation, and for those newly commissioned. Litany 3 or Litany 6 in The Book of Alternative Services *(pp. 112, 116) is appropriate.*

In Litany 3 the following may be inserted after the first petition.
We pray for this *parish* and for all who minister here (especially *N or NN*), that we may find joy in your service.
    Lord, hear our prayer.

In Litany 6 the following may be inserted after the first petition.

For the ministry of this *parish*, (and especially for *N or NN*), that we may b e a r faithful witness to the gospel of Christ, let us pray to the Lord.

Lord, have mercy.

The prayers may conclude with this collect.

Almighty God, by your grace alone
we are accepted and called to your service.
Strengthen us by your Holy Spirit and make us worthy of our calling;
through Jesus Christ our Lord,
who lives and reigns with you and the Holy Spirit,
one God, now and for ever.
  Amen.

*At the exchange of the Peace, the presiding minister and others may greet the newly
commissioned minister(s).*
  Service of Initiation (*Occasional Celebrations*, pages 112-113).

Appendix 2

Prayers for altar guild workers to be said before work

Lead us, O Lord, ever more deeply into the mysteries of life and death as we see
them revealed in the bread and wine of the Last Supper of thy Son Jesus Christ.
May we see there plainly, clearly, and simply stated, the meaning of our exist-
ence and thy purpose for us and all thy people everywhere. We ask this in the
name of Jesus who died that we might live.
  Amen.
  Theodore Ferris

We thank thee, O God, for the life and death of Jesus, his presence with us now;
help us to see him more clearly, to love him more dearly, and to follow him
more nearly, that his risen life may be in us; and as we die to the little things of
the world, may we live with him in light and love and life.
  Amen.
  Theodore Ferris

Open our minds, O God, and our spirits to the beauty and the truth of thy word
that it might light our path and ease our burden; and direct us through the
difficult and dangerous ways of our lives.
  Amen.
  Theodore Ferris

Grant me, I beseech thee, almighty and most merciful God, fervently to desire all things that are pleasing to thee; and of all that thou requirest me to do, grant me the knowledge, the desire, and the ability that I may so fulfil it as I ought, and my path to thee be straightforward to the end. Bestow upon me, O Lord, my God, understanding to know thee, diligence to seek thee, wisdom to find thee, and a faithfulness that may finally embrace thee.

Amen.

Thomas Aquinas

O God, who didst teach thy people of old to beautify and care for the holy place of thine abode; help us so to serve thee in thy sanctuaries here, that we may be numbered among those who worship before thy throne and see thy face hereafter; through the merits of Jesus Christ, thy Son, our Lord.

Amen.

Blessed are you, Shepherd of Israel, you lead your people like a flock. Strengthen me to care for your church in faithful integrity and gentle humility, for the sake of your Son, Jesus Christ our Lord.

Amen.

Occasional Celebrations

Prosper, O Lord, the work of our hand upon us, O prosper thou our handywork.

Amen.

Psalm 90:17

Appendix 3

Recipes for altar bread

Bread has always been an integral part of the eucharist, either in regular or wafer form. Wafers were introduced during the middle ages to prevent abuse to the sacrament; the Reformation assiduously abolished their use and reintroduced real bread. The wafer returned with the Oxford Movement of the nineteenth century. Today, the use of real bread for the eucharist is gradually returning; it is often made by members of the congregation and brought up to the altar at the offertory as the gifts of the people. Pita bread, which tears easily and leaves few crumbs is very appropriate and may be homemade or bought.

The following recipes are for homemade communion bread. Since none contains preservatives, the bread should be refrigerated or frozen if it is not used soon after baking.

Pita bread
   1 tablespoon (15 mL) yeast
   1/2 teaspoon (3 mL) sugar
   1 cup (230 mL) warm water
   2 tablespoons (30 mL) olive oil
   1 tablespoon (15 mL) salt
   3 cups (360 g) whole wheat or all-purpose flour

In a large bowl, dissolve the yeast in the sugar and water. Let the mixture sit for a few minutes until frothy. Add the oil, salt, and 2 1/2 cups of flour and beat well with a wooden spoon (dough will be sticky). Turn onto a floured surface and knead in the rest of the flour until the dough is elastic, smooth, and fairly firm. Shape into a ball and place in a buttered or lightly oiled bowl. Cover with a damp cloth and place in a warm place to rise for 1 1/2 to 2 hours until the dough doubles in size. Punch the dough down, turn it onto a floured board, cover, and let it rise for half an hour. Divide and shape the dough into 6-8 balls. Roll the balls out with a floured rolling pin to 1/4 inch (1/2 cm) thickness and into approximately 5 inch (13 cm) circles. Space well apart on cookie sheets, dust with flour, cover, and let rise for twenty minutes in a draft-free space. Bake at 500 F (260 C) on the bottom rack of the oven for five minutes. DO NOT OPEN THE OVEN DOOR. Transfer to a higher shelf for three minutes until the loaves are light brown and puffed up. Cover the loaves while they are cooling to deflate them and prevent them from turning crisp. Wrap quickly in plastic.

Whole wheat communion bread
   4 cups (480 g) whole wheat flour
   1 1/2 cups (350 mL) water
   2 1/2 teaspoons (12 mL) baking powder
   1/2 cup (120 mL) milk
   2 teaspoons (10 mL) salt
   1 tablespoon (15 mL) wheat germ

Dissolve salt and baking powder in the water. Add the wheat germ and the milk. Add the flour and stir well with a wooden spoon. Knead the dough for ten minutes on a floured board, adding flour or water as needed. Put the dough into a bowl, cover, and set aside for four hours. Shape the dough into loaves, four large or six small ones. Place on a greased cookie sheet. Bake for ten to fifteen minutes in a 375 F (180 C) oven.

Appendix 4

Further reading

Communion Bread
Begonja, Tony. *Eucharistic Bread Baking as Ministry*. San Jose, California: Resource Publications Inc., 1988.

Decorating the Church
Mazar, Peter. *To Crown the Year: Decorating the Church through the Seasons*. Liturgy Training Publications, 1995.

Flowers for the Church
Best, Margaret. *Growing and Arranging Church Flowers for Seasonal and Special Occasions*. London, Oxford: Mowbray, 1982.

Sayers, Susan. *Flowers for the Church Year - A Companion to the ASB*. Suffolk: Kevin Mayhew, Ltd., 1991.

Taylor, Jean. *Flowers in the Church*. London: Mowbray, 1976.

Linens, Hangings, and Vestments
Bradfield, Helen, et al. *Art of the Spirit*. Toronto & Oxford: Dundurn Press, 1992.

Dean, Beryl. *Church Embroidery*. Wilton, Connecticut: Morehouse Barlow, 1982.

_____, *Designing Ecclesiastical Stitched Textiles*. Tunbridge Wells: Burns and Oates/Search Press, 1993.

Joseph, Elizabeth. *Sewing Church Linens*. Harrisburg, PA: Morehouse Publishing, 1991.

Liddell, Jill. *The Patchwork Pilgrimage: How to Create Vibrant Church Vestments with Decoration*. New York: Viking Studio Books, 1993.

McNeill, Lucy. *Sanctuary Linens: Choosing, Making, and Embroidering*. Toronto: Anglican Book Centre, 1975.

Raynor, Louise, and Carolyn H. Kerr. *Church Needlepoint*, 2nd ed. Wilton, Connecticut: Morehouse, Barlow, 1989.

Thomson, Barbara, and Wendy Trewin. *Embroidered Church Kneelers*. London: B.T. Batsford, Ltd., 1987.

Wedge, Jeff. *Stole Patterns: Counted Cross Stitch*. Wilton, Connecticut: Morehouse, Barlow, 1986.

Index